rd,
water,
Wine
and
Bread

Illustrations by Bruce Sayre

WILLIAM H. WILLIMON

How Worship Has Changed over the Years

Judson Press ® Valley Forge

Word, Water, Wine and Bread

Copyright © 1980
Judson Press, Valley Forge, PA 19482-0851

Unless otherwise indicated, Bible quotations in this volume are from the
Revised Standard Version of the Bible, copyrighted 1946, 1952, 1971, 1973 © by the
Division of Christian Education of the National Council of the Churches of Christ
in the United States of America, and are used by permission.

Library of Congress Cataloging in Publication Data

Willimon, William H.
  Word, water, wine and bread.

  Includes bibliographical references.
  1. Liturgics—History. I. Title.
BV5.W54   264'.009   79-27661
ISBN 0-8170-0858-6

Printed in the U.S.A.
05 04 03 02 01
12 11 10 9

Contents

for
Stuart C. Henry
scholar, teacher, believer, friend

Introduction

When first published, this book heralded a momentous change in the history of the way Christians praise God. Today, two decades after it appeared, *Word, Water, Wine, and Bread* provides the rationale for what most Christians have experienced every Sunday in our churches. That this book has found a place in the curriculum of a dozen theological seminaries in a wide array of Catholic, Protestant, and Free Church seminaries not only pleased me, but also testified to worship renewal as that which united us beyond our differences.

Among Roman Catholics since Vatican II and in most mainline Protestant denominations, Sunday morning worship has changed more in the past thirty years than in the past four hundred. Liturgical innovation is no longer the hope of a few specialists—it is now a fact of life for the average congregation.

In the first edition, I sympathized with those pastors and lay persons who were dismayed by innovations in their accustomed worship practices. Part of the power of the liturgy is its predictability, sameness, uniformity, and familiar words and gestures. Many Roman Catholics, who once saw the Mass as an unchangeable bulwark amidst a sea of change, felt that the church had pulled up anchor and was hopelessly adrift. The United Methodist who was comfortable with the old, restrained sobriety of the "Service of Holy Communion," when confronted with a more joyful sacrament of the Lord's Supper, might exclaim with John Wesley, "I like the old wine best!" Conservative Lutherans, long nurtured on nonsacrificial Communions, found that when they participated in the new services of the Inter-Lutheran Commission on Worship they recalled Luther's rebuke of some liturgical innovators in his day who "act like unclean swine, rush wildly about and rejoice only in the novel, and as soon as the novelty has worn off forthwith become disgusted with it." [1]

Today, many congregations are locked in "the worship wars" as they battle over "traditional" versus "contemporary" worship styles. Some attempt "blended worship," hoping to strike a balance between guitars and pipe organs. In church after church, arguments over worship continue to be the most divisive issue within the congregation. When we opened the floodgates to liturgical reform, we let loose a deluge.

Whence did this worship innovation and liturgical experimentation come? The sources are many and the factors complex: a desire to adapt our worship to the needs and realities of the contemporary church, ecumenism, pluralism, ethnic awareness, and dissatisfaction with the theological and biblical shallowness of most Protestant worship. A main source of our most radical worship innovation has come from our discovery of our *past* in worship. In our uniquely "a-historical" milieu, sometimes the oldest truths have a strikingly contemporary ring. Modern liturgical experimentation has often found that the path to meaningful liturgy requires us to journey again where the church has been before in order that we might arrive where we would like to be today.

Karl Barth said that what matters most in the church's worship is not

---

[1] Martin Luther, "An Order of Mass and Communion for the Church at Wittenberg," from *Luther's Works*, ed. Ulrich S. Leupold, trans. Paul Z. Strodach (Philadelphia: Fortress Press, 1964), vol. 53, p. 19.

being up to date, but *reformation*. Reformation does not mean to go with the times or let the spirit of the age judge what is true and false. It means to carry out better than yesterday the task of singing a new song unto the Lord. "It means never to grow tired of returning not to the origin in time but to the origin in substance of the community."[2] Or as Pius XII said in his encyclical on worship, "To return in mind and heart to the well-springs of the sacred liturgy..."[3] This is the purpose of this book: to recall where we have been in Christian worship so that we might see better where we ought to be going.

For many of us Protestants, worship is a relatively new concern. We have neglected liturgical study in our seminaries and have been haphazard in the worship life of our local congregations. This book is an invitation to liturgical history for clergy, seminarians, and some lay persons. Because I have a United Methodist background, the book attempts to do justice to both Catholic and the Evangelical Free Church traditions, since United Methodists have roots in both. The book's title is an indication of its primary focus—the history of Sunday morning worship through the preached Word and through baptism and the Lord's Supper as practiced in the Western church.

I want to thank again my former churches where I led worship; my students at Duke Divinity School who heard and reacted to most of this material in my introductory worship course; Mrs. M. M. Martin, my secretary; Dr. Stuart Henry and Dr. James May, who read various parts of this book while it was in progress; and the Reverend Bruce Sayre who did the illustrations.

Through this book, I hope that our rich heritage of Word, water, wine and bread will come alive for you. Our liturgical history is nothing less than the story of how God has been and continues to be with us. The words, traditionally spoken by the priest, inviting people to the Lord's Table, express the essence of our worship, past and present:

"The Gifts of God for the People of God!"
To which gifts the people respond, "Amen!"

Duke University
Durham, North Carolina
Pentecost, 2001

[2] Karl Barth, *Church Dogmatics* (New York: Charles Scribner's Sons, 1956), vol. 4, part 1, p. 705.

[3] Pius XII, Encyclical *Mediator Dei*, 20 November 1947.

Fresco "Consecration of the Tabernacle,"
Synagogue at Dura-Europas, A.D. 245

The Jewish Heritage: Tabernacle, Temple, Synagogue, Dinner Table

1

Before we were Christians, we were Jews. Jesus was a Jew. The faith he proclaimed was born of two thousand years of nomadic wandering, Egyptian slavery, kingly rule, Babylonian exile, and Roman occupation. Christian worship was built, to a great extent, upon Jewish rites that already existed, even if the inner meaning of those rites was dramatically transformed by the first Christians.

Tabernacle

Amidst primordial nomadic origins, the tabernacle was born—a portable sanctuary, a "tent of meeting" which Moses erected in the wilderness to house the ark of the covenant and the throne of Yahweh. While our descriptions of the tabernacle (Exodus 25-31; 35-40) are probably the idealized backward look of later priestly writers into a dim past, those descriptions give us a sense of the nature of early Jewish worship. Here Yahweh "tabernacled," or "tented," with Israel:

"There I will meet with the people of Israel. . . . I will dwell among the people of Israel, and will be their God. And they shall know that I am [Yahweh] their God, who brought them forth out of the land of Egypt that I might dwell among them. . . ." (Exodus 29:43-46a).

Exodus depicts Yahweh instructing Moses to build this tent of goat hair to enclose such cultic furnishings as a table of shewbread, altar of incense, golden candlestick, and, behind the veil in the holy of holies, the ark of the covenant containing the tablets of the Law. Surrounding the tabernacle was a large enclosed court where burnt offerings were sacrificed and where a gigantic bronze laver of obscure symbolism and function stood.

For ancient Israel, worship meant to "draw near." The interior architectural arrangement of the tabernacle reflected degrees of access to the holy. At the center in the holy of holies was the mercy seat of Yahweh above the ark. Outside the veil was the less holy place, the court for public sacrifices, then the dwellings of the priests, and then the main encampment. Likewise, varying degrees of holiness were reflected in the diminishing value of the metals used: fine gold for the ark itself, bronze for the laver in the outer court. The court was accessible to the people; the holy place in the tabernacle could be entered only by priests; the holy of holies was entered only by the high priest once a year. These spatial and cultic expressions of the nearness, distance, and approachability of the divine are typical of the worship of Israel.

Temple

As the Jewish nation became established, the tabernacle's arrangements for meeting Yahweh were made more permanent. By definition, the holy cannot be defined or limited; but humanity naturally wants some place, some definite locus for its encounters with the divine. The temple which came to be built in Jerusalem was possibly an elaboration of the primal tabernacle. Three successive temples rose on the same site in Jerusalem: Solomon's temple, so magnificent that it eventually bankrupted the kingdom (c. 957 B.C.); Zerubbabel's crude, short-lived imitation (c. 515 B.C.); and, finally, Herod's temple, the temple that Jesus knew (destroyed A.D. 70).

What was worship in the temple like? Isaiah describes a stirring experience of temple worship sometime around 742 B.C.:

> In the year that King Uzziah died I saw the Lord sitting upon a throne, high and lifted up; and his train filled the temple. Above him stood the seraphim; each had six wings: with two he covered his face, and with two he covered his feet, and with two he flew. And one called to another and said:
> "Holy, holy, holy is the LORD of hosts;
> the whole earth is full of his glory."
> And the foundations of the thresholds shook at the voice of him who called, and the house was filled with smoke. And I said: "Woe is me! For I am lost; for I am a man of unclean lips, . . . for my eyes have seen the King, the LORD of hosts!"
> Then flew one of the seraphim to me, having in his hand a burning coal which he had taken with tongs from the altar. And he touched my mouth, and said: "Behold, this has touched your lips; your guilt is taken away, and your sin forgiven." And I heard the voice of the Lord saying, "Whom shall I send, and who will go for us?" Then I said, "Here am I! Send me" (Isaiah 6:1-8).

Even though this passage may not describe an experience within an actual service, it does give us a feel for one worshiper's experience in the temple. It was once popular to speak of this "Isaiah motif" as a possible pattern for ordering the various acts of Christian worship. The passage shows progression from (1) *Adoration*, "Holy, holy . . .," to (2) *Confession*, "Woe is me . . .," to (3) *Forgiveness*, "Your guilt is taken away and your sin forgiven," to (4) *Proclamation*, "I heard the voice of the Lord saying . . .," and finally to (5) *Dedication*, "Here am I! Send me." While this is a questionable pattern for full Christian worship, Isaiah's experience in the temple shows both the transcendent and the ethical dimensions that are part of the Jewish faith.

One of the best contemporary descriptions of worship in the temple is a passage in the apocryphal book of the Wisdom of Jesus the Son of Sirach (usually referred to as Ecclesiasticus or Sirach). It describes a service led by the high priest Simon II (c. 220-195 B.C.):

When he put on his glorious robe
  and clothed himself with superb perfection
and went up to the holy altar,
  he made the court of the sanctuary glorious.
And when he received the portions from the
    hands of the priests,
    as he stood by the hearth of the altar
with a garland of brethren around him,
  he was like a young cedar on Lebanon;
and they surrounded him like the trunks of
    palm trees,
    all the sons of Aaron in their splendor
with the Lord's offering in their hands,
  before the whole congregation of Israel.
Finishing the service at the altars,
  and arranging the offering to the Most High,
    the Almighty,
he reached out his hand to the cup
  and poured a libation of the blood of the
    grape;
he poured it out at the foot of the altar,
  a pleasing odor to the Most High, the King
    of all.
Then the sons of Aaron shouted,
  they sounded the trumpets of hammered work,
they made a great noise to be heard
  for remembrance before the Most High.
Then all the people together made haste
  and fell to the ground upon their faces
to worship their Lord,
  the Almighty, God Most High.
And the singers praised him with their voices
  in sweet and full-toned melody.
And the people besought the Lord Most High
  in prayer before him who is merciful,
till the order of worship of the Lord was ended;
  so they completed his service.
Then Simon came down, and lifted up his hands
  over the whole congregation of the sons
    of Israel,

to pronounce the blessing of the Lord with his
   lips,
and to glory in his name;
and they bowed down in worship a second time,
to receive the blessing from the Most High.
                                    —Sirach 50:11-21

A hierarchical priesthood presided over sacrifices *(zebach)* at the Jerusalem temple. While there were many varieties of sacrifices, a common ritual pattern can be seen in the many Old Testament descriptions. First, there was preparation as the worshipers cleansed themselves for the ritual and then prepared a perfect animal for butchering. The animal was offered to Yahweh as a gift of the worshiper, not in the sense of "giving up" something nor in the sense of giving up something in order to obtain a greater reward (which our present uses of the word "sacrifice" often denote) but in the Jewish sense of a freely given gift to the God who is the Giver of all gifts. Then the animal was butchered, and certain parts were burned upon the altar. While the death of the animal was a necessary preliminary part of the sacrifice, the killing itself was never the central act of the sacrifice, nor was the death of the victim imbued with any special significance. The death of the animal was not the sacrifice; it was only a necessary part of the *gift* of the sacrifice. Finally, there was a joyful feast upon the animal's flesh shared by priests and people. *This* was the central act, *a feast shared by humans and God.*

While none of these sacrificial activities carried over into Christianity or modern Judaism, the inner meaning of the sacrificial rites remained central to Judeo-Christian religion: acknowledgment of devotion to and dependence upon God and the joyful offering of the stuff of everyday life as a thankful acknowledgment of God's love and grace.

Synagogue

The ancient Jews show little development of the visual arts. But in the arts of the Word—in the development, loving nurture, and respect for poetry, history, law, narrative, and preaching—they had few equals. They were "People of the Book." The Torah, the law, contained the day-to-day, minutely detailed dealings of God with God's Chosen People.

The People of the Book gathered themselves around an

institution known as the synagogue. There is no mention of the synagogue in the Old Testament, and its origin is disputed. The most common hypothesis is that synagogue gatherings arose during the exilic period after the destruction of the temple in 587 B.C. With the temple's destruction and dispersal of the Jewish people, a new form of worship and community life was needed. The synagogue arose to meet the needs of the times.

Through the synagogues, located in any community where there were at least ten Jewish men, the scribes and Pharisees gained great influence over the people, cultivating the ritualism of sabbath regulations and cultic requirements. Pharisaism, with its complex regulations and stress upon strict personal adherence to the Law, is an expression of the temple-synagogue cultus of Jesus' day. While the Pharisees have received admittedly "bad press" in the Christian Gospels, the elaborate, minutely "rubricized" ritual which the Pharisees advocated represents a key Jewish belief that the law—pervading every aspect of daily life, defying the boundaries between "secular" and "sacred"—is the gift of a gracious God who does not leave the people of God without daily guidance and a prescribed pathway to righteousness. Worship in the synagogue reinforced the everyday, mundane, worldly piety which has been the genius of Judaism.

The synagogue served many purposes in the life of a Jewish community. It was first and foremost a school. On the sabbath and other holy days it was a place of worship. In the synagogue many Jews began to see the study of Scripture and the offering of prayer rather than sacrifice as the heart of worship. Two great Jewish ideals were linked in the synagogue: worship and education.

With the destruction of the last temple in A.D. 70, the synagogue became the principal religious institution in Judaism. "Synagogue" comes from the Greek sunagoge, meaning "gathering place, assembly, congregation, meeting," which is the Greek rendering of the Hebrew edah, "congregation." Synagogue services were led by several people, mostly laymen. Jesus' first sermon as recorded in Luke gives us a glimpse of synagogue worship in the first century and a picture of Jesus as rabbi (Luke 4:16-27). The Shema was recited: "Hear, O Israel: The Lord our God is one Lord; and you shall love the Lord your God with all your heart, and with all your soul, and with all your mind, and with all your strength" (see Deuteronomy 6:4-9; 11:13-21). The

Shema was followed by benedictions, "Bless the Lord . . .," and then lessons from the Torah were read in sequential course. Read as *lectio continua*, the entire Torah was read once every three years or as an annual cycle. After the Torah, the Haftorah, or Prophets, was read, with interpretations and homilies upon these lessons. Any visiting rabbi could be invited to interpret the lessons (see Acts 13:5), and Luke records the uproar Jesus created when he interpreted during his visit to his hometown synagogue.

The introduction of the temple psalms into synagogue worship is a matter of dispute. Some authorities believe that certain psalms were sung in the synagogue at an early date; others see the use of psalms as a late development, perhaps long after they were used by Christians in their worship. At any rate, there is little doubt of the great influence of the form and content of synagogue worship in general on the liturgical life of the early church.

The Gospels depict Jesus as frequenting the synagogues as well as the temple of Herod. Luke says that Jesus was brought to the temple as an infant for his presentation and as a boy during Passover (Luke 2:22-52). He was there for the Feast of the Tabernacles (John 7:2) and for Hanukkah, or the Feast of Dedication (John 10:22). Jesus' confrontation with the money changers (Matthew 21:12) and his criticisms of the temple sacrifices (Matthew 9:13) cannot be seen as condemnations of temple worship *per se* but, rather, as criticisms of abuses of the cult, very much like the criticisms of Old Testament prophets like Hosea before him. Perhaps his deep reverence for his Father's house led him to criticize mercenary and exclusivistic abuses of the temple.

The book of Acts shows Peter, Paul, and John in the temple and the early Christians in the temple and synagogue. Perhaps the recorded attacks of Jesus upon the cultic system were the products of Jewish Christians who had to come to terms with the problem of the destruction of the temple in A.D. 70 and their expulsion from the synagogues as Christianity developed:

". . . the hour [comes and is now] when neither on this mountain nor in Jerusalem will you worship the Father . . . true worshipers will worship the Father in spirit and truth" (John 4:21-23*a*).

Only later in his ministry (Galatians 4:10ff.; Colossians 2:16) does Paul protest against the sabbath as an abridgment of Christian freedom.

Even though Christians gradually abandoned worship in the temple and synagogue, synagogue patterns were to have lasting influence on Christian worship. By the end of the first century, Christians were to have a liturgy directly derived from synagogue worship. They called it by the Greek word *synaxis,* which comes from the same root as "synagogue" and which means "meeting." The *synaxis,* or Service of the Word, consisted of the following elements which have an obvious parallel to synagogue worship:

Synaxis (A.D. 150-200)

1. Greeting by president
2. Readings and Psalms
3. Sermon
4. Dismissal of unbaptized
5. Prayers of the church
6. The peace
7. (Dismissal of the church on weekdays when the Lord's Supper is not celebrated)

Dinner Table

Finally, the Jewish religion had a fourth locus of worship—the dinner table. For the Jew, *every* meal had great religious significance. To "prepare a table for me in the midst of mine enemies," as in Psalm 23, would be seen by the Jew as an act of deep friendship. The person who invites you to dinner is the person who sticks by you at all costs. For Jesus to be at the dinner table with sinners and publicans would be seen as a public declaration of scandalous solidarity with the outcasts, a very different vision of the expected Great Banquet of the Messiah (Isaiah 55).

The Passover *(pesach)* was the most important Jewish religious meal. It is of interest to Christians because Jesus was crucified during Passover. The Synoptic Gospels identify the Last Supper with the Passover (Matthew 26:17; Mark 14:12; Luke 22:7, 15), and Paul even spoke of Christ as "our Passover" (1 Corinthians 5:7-8).

The Passover festival is at least twenty-five hundred years old. It is celebrated on the first full moon of the Hebrew year as a spring lamb is offered to Yahweh. While the Passover probably began as an agricultural festival, it became associated with the Exodus from

Egypt. To the present day, the seder (the order of worship which is used at the Passover feast) proclaims:

> We were Pharaoh's slaves in Egypt, and the Lord our God brought us forth from there with a mighty hand and an outstretched arm. And if the Holy One, blessed be he, had not brought our forefathers forth from Egypt, then we, our children, and our children's children would still be Pharaoh's slaves in Egypt.[1]

In the Passover seder God's mighty act of deliverance is remembered and celebrated, not simply as a historical commemoration, but in a way in which the participants become part of this deliverance themselves through the meal. In eating and remembering, they are themselves redeemed:

> In every generation let each man look on himself as if *he* came forth out of Egypt.
> As it is said: "And thou shalt tell thy son in that day, saying: It is because of that which the Lord did for me when I came forth out of Egypt". . . .
> It was not only our fathers that the Holy One, blessed be he, redeemed, but us as well did he redeem along with them. . . .

> He has brought us forth from slavery to freedom, from sorrow to joy, from mourning to holiday, from darkness to great light, and from bondage to redemption.[2]

The central activity of the Passover meal is the offering and the eating of a roast lamb. The lamb must be eaten in haste, as if it were being eaten by fleeing nomads. The flesh is totally consumed, an act which became interpreted later as a sign of complete trust in and total dependence upon Yahweh. Blood from the lamb is used to mark the door of the house in order to purify the house where the sacrifice is eaten (Exodus 12:23). As in other Jewish sacrifices, no special significance was attached to the death of the lamb. The focus was, rather, upon the grace of God who nourishes and delivers God's people, a grace which was particularly evident in the Exodus, a grace which Christians were to see in the Christ.

By the time of Christ, another festival, which probably originated as an ancient agricultural feast celebrating the new crop

[1] Nahum N. Glatzer, ed., *The Passover Haggadah* (New York: Schocken Books, Inc., 1969), p. 23. Reprinted by permission of Schocken Books, Inc. from *The Passover Haggadah*, edited by Nahum N. Glatzer. Copyright © 1953, 1969, 1979 by Schocken Books, Inc.
[2] *Ibid.*, pp. 49, 51.

and the new year, became associated with the Passover—the Feast of Unleavened Bread. This feast, lasting eight days, was linked to the *pesach* in Exodus 12:39 and became associated with deliverance and renewal. The unleavened bread reminded the Passover participants of the bread which was taken into the wilderness in haste, before the bread had time to rise.

While the Passover is the central Jewish religious meal, every sabbath and every feast was an occasion for a religious meal. We are not sure whether the meal which Jesus ate with his disciples at the Last Supper was a Passover meal or an ordinary religious meal, since the scriptural accounts differ. But it is clear that he died during Passover week and that the meaning of this festival of deliverance became associated with deliverance through the death and resurrection of Christ.

In the scriptural accounts of the Last Supper Jesus makes no use of the specific Passover ceremonies which we noted above. His blessing of the bread and the cup are typical of other meals, such as the sabbath meals.

In the sabbath meal, after the sabbath candles are lighted and all are seated, a cup of wine is poured and a *kiddush*, or blessing, is recited:

Blessed art thou, O Lord our God, King of the universe who createst the fruit of the vine.

This is the blessing which Luke may have had in mind when he says that Jesus ". . . took a cup, and when he had given thanks . . ." (Luke 22:17-18).

Following the blessing over the cup is the blessing of bread:

Blessed art thou, O Lord our God, King of the universe who bringest forth bread from the earth.

At the sabbath meal, the father holds the bread in his hands while saying this blessing. Then he breaks the bread and gives it to the participants, eating a piece of it himself. It was at this point that Jesus probably said, "This is my body."

The blessings over the bread and cup marked the formal beginning of the meal. During the meal there was conversation and fellowship which were themselves part of the "sacredness" of every meal. During Jesus' day, *chaburah* (small groups of friends who formed religious societies around a distinguished rabbi) would meet and eat and engage in religious discussions. Some have suggested that rabbi Jesus and his disciples may have constituted such a *chaburah*. At any rate, it was this familylike, domestic gathering of family and friends which set the tone for every Jewish festival and which Christians saw as particularly expressive of their own experience of the risen Christ.

At the close of the meal, a prayer is said over a final cup of wine, "the cup of blessing" to which Paul refers (1 Corinthians 10:16). It is introduced by a dialogue. Then a series of blessings, thanksgivings, and petitions follows. This is probably the "cup after supper" of Luke 22:20 and 1 Corinthians 11:25. During this prayer the father holds the cup in both hands and lifts it. After the prayer, all the wine is drunk by the participants. In this "cup of blessing" and its accompanying prayer, we probably have the source of what would become the eucharistic prayer, or prayer of thanksgiving, of Christians.

While the early Christians broke with their Jewish forebears and Christian worship radically reinterpreted the purpose and theology of liturgy, Christians responded to their new revelation through inherited worship forms. The Christian *synaxis* (Service of the Word) with its reading and expounding of Scripture and its historical recitation of "the mighty acts of God" came from the synagogue. The church year, our ordering of time and liturgical seasons like Pentecost (the Jewish Feast of Weeks) and Easter (the Jewish Passover) came from the Jewish calendar. Our ritual use of water, oil, bread, and wine have obvious antecedents in Jewish rites. The Christian Eucharist, or Lord's Supper, and the form and focus of the eucharistic prayer were adapted from the Jewish table fellowship. The Psalter was our first hymnbook.

Tabernacle, temple, synagogue, and dinner table together express the dialectical facets of Jewish worship: sacrificial and ethical, institutional and prophetic, transcendent and immanent, public and domestic, historical and eschatological. To worship as Christians in the light of our Scripture and heritage, these dialectical aspects, these rich emphases from our Jewish past, should be expressed in our worship today if the God we worship is truly the God of Abraham, Isaac, and Jacob—and Jesus.

Tomb fresco "Celestial Banquet,"
Cemetery of Cyriaca, 3rd century

Bread, Wine, Water: The Lord's Supper and Baptism in New Testament Times

2

At the dawn of the New Age we find the *ecclesia*, the church, gathering on Sunday for communal meals of great significance. For a while, Jewish Christians continued to worship in their synagogues and the temple. But by the end of the first century it was apparent that Christianity represented a different vision of worship, which made its eventual break with Judaism inevitable.

Christians, rather than retaining the Jewish sabbath, worshiped on the first day of the week—the day of creation, light, Pentecost (the birthday of the church), the day of the resurrection of Christ. "The Lord's Day," the early Christians believed, represent-

ed the New Age which had dawned with its new eschatological
ordering of life and time.

The numerous liturgical fragments which crop up throughout the New Testament—such as the hymns the "Magnificat"
(Luke 1:46-55), the "Benedictus" (1:68-79), the "Nunc Dimittis"
(2:29-32), and the "Kenosis" hymn (Philippians 2:6-11)—remind
us that the New Testament was first a compilation of a diverse oral
tradition for use in the context of Sunday worship. John 6:35-50
could well be used as an early sermon for the Lord's Supper. The
book of Revelation, a vision "on the Lord's day" (Revelation 1:10),
contains prayers, hymns, and actions which may have been parts of
a first-century Sunday service.

Bread and Wine

There is no one New Testament view of early Christian
worship. The liturgical picture of the early church is one of
diversity rather than uniformity. The free operation of the Spirit
within the church manifested itself in a variety of ways: preaching,
prophecy, speaking in tongues, baptism, and intercessory prayer.
However, on the basis of New Testament evidence, it is reasonable
to assume that the primary context for these various acts of worship
was the weekly Sunday evening gathering for the Lord's Supper.

Jesus shared many religiously significant meals with his
disciples. Luke–Acts records Jesus at a series of meals, each of
which revealed an important aspect of his message and ministry.
At supper with Levi (Luke 5:29-39) Jesus is criticized for eating
with sinners and for the joyful nature of his table fellowship. The
accusation that Jesus is a "glutton and a wine drinker who eats
with sinners" (see Luke 7:34) is well documented by Luke (7:36-50;
11:37-52; 14:1-24). In these mealtime episodes Jesus is at odds with
many of the Pharisaic barriers between "sinners" and the
"righteous" as well as with much of the law itself ("Why do your
disciples eat with unwashed hands?" [Mark 7:1-8]). One might also
recall the joyous party at the homecoming of the prodigal son
(Luke 15:11-24), where the meal is a sign of reconciliation, or the
miracle of the feeding of the five thousand (Luke 9:10-17), where
the meal is related to "feeding" (a rich and multifaceted image) the
hungry and suffering multitudes. Luke's account of the Passover
meal in Luke 22:14-38 becomes an occasion for Jesus' most
important teaching on sin, repentance, and forgiveness and is the

only meal in Luke where Jesus is both servant and host. This final meal before the crucifixion is also eaten with sinners, though they be sinners and betrayers who are also disciples.

The meal Jesus ate with his disciples in the upper room was not the "last" supper, for there is the Emmaus meal (Luke 24:13-35), bringing Luke's Gospel to a climax, where the shattered faith of the disciples is transformed "when he was at the table with them" and "their eyes were opened" to the presence of the risen Christ. In the Emmaus experience the Scriptures are made known; understanding, disclosure, and recognition are given to the disciples. A final significant meal in Luke–Acts is Acts 2:42 where "the breaking of bread" becomes the seal and the testimony of the power of the Pentecost experience and the birthday of the church. The prophets had foretold that the Messiah would begin the banquet of the Lord. The vision of sinners and all nations eating together at Pentecost becomes proof of the initiation of the messianic age in Jesus' name.

And they, continuing daily with one accord in the temple, and breaking bread from house to house, did eat their meat with gladness and singleness of heart, praising God, and having favour with all the people. And the Lord added to the church daily such as should be saved (Acts 2:46-47, KJV).

The precise form of these sacred meals of the early Christians has been debated for many years. At what time did the early "breaking of bread" become the carefully defined rite that emerges by the end of the second century? The question is complicated because the seemingly nonspecific instruction "to break bread," or a corresponding phrase, is found in a number of accounts: Matthew 14:19; 15:36; Luke 24:35; Acts 2:42; 20:7; 27:35; 1 Corinthians 10:16; 11:24. In Jude, verse 12, and 2 Peter 2:13 (see footnote in Revised Standard Version) there are references to a meal called the "agape" ("love feast"). But in First Corinthians, where Paul is undoubtedly speaking of a specific liturgical meal, the term "Lord's Supper" is used. The variety of terms suggests that the sacred meal was undergoing a process of development during this early period, a process which would coalesce by the end of the second century in a more formal and schematized table ritual.

Seven-Action Pattern

Most scholars believe that, at the very beginning of the church,

Christians celebrated a full common meal (the agape?) with prayers of blessing (*eucharistia*—Greek for "thanksgiving") patterned after the Jewish table blessings and prayed before and after the meal. The pattern was thus much the same as the sacred meals in Judaism: (1) taking bread, (2) thanking God, (3) breaking bread, (4) giving the bread, (5) taking the wine after the meal, (6) thanking God, and (7) giving the wine. Perhaps because of paganistic confusion of the meaning of this meal with the meaning of sacred meals in the Mysteries, or the problem of accommodating larger crowds at the meals, or abuses of the meal, the table ceremonial became a more schematized, self-contained, ritual meal while the full meal or agape continued as a separate entity rather than as the original intervening meal between the opening and closing blessings. In other words, the full meal dropped out, leaving the opening and closing table ceremonial which now became known as the Eucharist, or Lord's Supper.

First Corinthians, chapter 11, probably describes a meal at which the full meal and the Eucharist were still combined ("Likewise, after supper he took the cup and blessed it and said . . ."). Among the Corinthians, abuses arose from pride, enthusiastic excesses, and paganistic syncretism which had apparently fragmented the Corinthian church into opposing factions. Paul tells them that they think they are eating the "Lord's Supper" *(kurakon diepnon)* when, in reality, they have splintered into their own private meals *(idion diepnon)* which, because of a lack of love and ethical responsibility, are the antithesis of what Christ instituted (vv. 23-25) and a violation of the "body" (v. 29)—the "body" being the church, the "body of Christ" in Pauline theology (see Romans 12). Christian table fellowship has been lost in selfish debauchery.

Some have suggested that the Corinthians, caught up in individualistic enthusiasm, confused the Christian meal with the magical food of their old pagan mystery religions. The bread and the wine had become objects of superstitious idolatry which were eaten for magical protection. This, Paul seems to be saying, is at odds with the Christian understanding of the Lord's Supper as a joyful corporate meal which expresses the communion of those who gather in Jesus' name. Paul's injunction about "discerning the body" does not have to do with the elements of bread and wine. Rather, "the body" is the usual Pauline symbol for the church. To "discern the body" means to see one's brothers and sisters around the table as the visible presence of the risen Christ. The Corinthians are "eating and drinking their own destruction" because of their selfish behavior at the very meal which is itself a model of Christ's own self-giving. The matter under debate is, therefore, as much a question of ethics as a question of worship. Perhaps 2 Peter 2:13 and Jude 12 are responses to similar abuses of the Lord's Supper.

Was the Lord's Supper a continuation of the Emmaus-type resurrection meal or a commemoration of the Last Supper before crucifixion? Perhaps the best we can say is that, at an early date, the Supper was interpreted both as a remembrance of the sacrifice of "Christ our Passover" and also as a joyous thanksgiving *(eucharistia)* for the victory of the resurrection.

A paschal remembrance of our Passover from death to life, a symbol of fellowship in Christ, a joyful foretaste of the messianic banquet, a paradigm for Christian life; the Lord's Supper was, from the first, a multifaceted, multidimensional experience of Christian worship.

Four-Action Pattern

As the church moved into the third century, a dramatic change occurred in Christian worship as the once full meal with its seven-action pattern was compressed into a more schematized four-action pattern of (1) taking bread and wine, (2) thanking God over the bread and wine, (3) breaking the bread, and (4) giving bread and wine. The Lord's Supper was separated from the full meal and acquired this format with which we are familiar today. In some Christian communities the full meal probably continued for a time as a fellowship meal and an occasion to care for the poor.

Water

John the Baptist prepared the way by preaching a baptism of repentance as a sign of a new beginning and incorporation into a new eschatological community of the repentant. "Get washed up in order to be ready for the New Age that is coming," was John's message. Jesus' submission to baptism by John is a prelude to the significant part this symbolic act was to play in the practice of the faith.

The ritual use of water for purificatory purposes is common to nearly every religion. Water had long been used by the Jews for purification rites associated with temple worship (Leviticus 15:5, 8, 13; Exodus 30:19-20). The Jews also practiced proselyte baptism in which Gentiles, who wished to become Jews, were instructed in the Law and the Jewish heritage, circumcised if they were males, then baptized into the house of Israel by immersion in running water. The extent to which Jewish proselyte baptism influenced Christian baptism is not known. There is no mention of such baptisms until about A.D. 200. Early Christian baptismal initiations may have had some relation to the baptisms of the first-century Jewish sects whose members frequently purified themselves by bathing, but the relationship has never been established.

Rather than looking for a foreshadowing of the Christian rite within these Jewish ceremonial washings, it is more fruitful to focus upon the nature of membership in the old Israel as it relates to Christian beliefs about membership in the new Israel. It is here that we see a Jewish background for Christian baptism.

Membership in the nation of Israel was not a matter of nature or birth *per se*. Israel had been "no people"; but Yahweh chose Israel, began a covenant with them, and formed them into a "holy people." Circumcision was the rite of initiation into this covenant. One was not born a Jew, but made a Jew through the incorporating act of circumcision. In the new Israel (the church) baptism is not described as circumcision until the deutero-Pauline book of Colossians (2:11-12). But the idea that one becomes a member of the new covenant community only by being ritually initiated into that community hark back to Jewish circumcision.

Initiation

The early Christians eventually dropped the practice of circumcision because it was too nationalistic, excluded women from full membership, and related too closely to the cultic requirements of the old covenant. Baptism, in the form of, if not with the same meaning as, Jewish baptismal practices, became the rite of initiation into the Christian community. We have little evidence regarding New Testament baptismal practice. It was probably, like Jewish proselyte baptisms, baptism in the nude by immersion in running water. Arguments over whether it was "infant" or "adult" baptism are more related to later theological controversies than biblical evidence. It is reasonable to assume that early baptisms were missionary baptisms of adult converts. Like Jewish proselyte baptism, sometimes entire households, including children, were baptized when the master of the house accepted the Christian faith (see Acts 16:15; 18:8; 1 Corinthians 1:16). By the second century, baptism of the infant children of Christian parents was an accepted practice. Infant baptism did not become an officially sanctioned practice until well into the fourth century. The age of the baptismal candidate or mode of baptism are not discussed in the New Testament. The meaning of baptism more than the mode is the New Testament's concern. Just as the Lord's Supper has a range of self-evident meanings that are inherent in any meal, so baptism incorporates all the symbolic meaning of water: creation, birth, life, death, and cleansing. Baptism meant all these things in the New Testament church.

In Acts, Christian baptism is spoken of with three connotations: "for the forgiveness of sins," "into the name of Christ," and "you shall receive the Holy Spirit." The baptism of the Holy Spirit, while appearing to be rather loosely attached to baptism in Acts, was an integral part of water baptism. Phrases like "putting on Christ," "adoption," "new birth," "holy nation," and "death and resurrection" are often used in later New Testament writings in reference to baptism. Note this portion of what may have been an early baptismal hymn:

Once [we] were no people
but now [we] are God's people;
Once [we] had not received mercy
but now [we] have received mercy.
—1 Peter 2:10

Paul uses the Hellenistic Christian idea of baptism as death—dying to the old person and rising in the new. Jesus himself had referred to baptism as death (Mark 10:39). Paul, in writing to the Romans on the ethical implications of baptism, says:

Do you not know that all of us who have been baptized into Christ Jesus were baptized into his death? We were buried therefore with him by baptism into death, so that as Christ was raised from the dead by the glory of the Father, we too might walk in newness of life (Romans 6:3-4).

Conversion into the faith, initiation into God's holy nation, is nothing less than death itself; it is a radical break with the old life and a radical incorporation into new life, as radical an act as the death and resurrection of Christ himself. Paul says that through baptism we are linked to Christ's own dying and rising. We are "buried" in the baptismal waters. Then we rise to "walk in newness of life."

Elsewhere, in a passage that may have been part of an early baptismal liturgy, Paul speaks of baptism as the basis for Christian unity:

In Christ Jesus [we] are all sons of God, through faith.
For [we who] were baptized into Christ have put on Christ.
There is neither Jew nor Greek,
there is neither slave nor free,
there is neither male nor female;
for [we] are all one in Christ. . . .

—Galatians 3:26-28

The cleansing waters of baptism wash away all racial, social, and sexual distinctions which characterized life in the Old Age.

Above all, baptism was Christian initiation. It marked the entrance into a new eschatological community gathered in the name of Christ. It was an objective act with subjective effects. Just as the Israelites passed, by God's grace, through the Red Sea from slavery to freedom to become God's people (1 Corinthians 10:2), so we pass through the waters of baptism from death to life (1 Corinthians 10:2) to become God's people in the church. We go under the waters, dying to the old sin and bondage and rising to righteousness and freedom. Once again, to quote from an early baptismal hymn:

[We are] built into a spiritual house,
    to be a holy priesthood,
    to offer spiritual sacrifices
    acceptable to God through . . . Christ.
[We] are a chosen race,
    a royal priesthood,
    a holy nation,
    God's own people,
that [we] may declare the wonderful deeds
    of him who called [us] out of darkness
    into his [own] marvelous light.

—1 Peter 2:5, 9

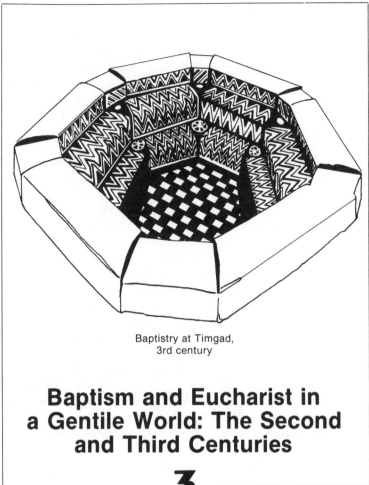

Baptistry at Timgad,
3rd century

Baptism and Eucharist in a Gentile World: The Second and Third Centuries

3

During its first century, the church struggled to define itself in relation to its Jewish origins. In the next two centuries the church fought to maintain its integrity as it confronted the diverse cultures, philosophies, and religions of the Greco-Roman world. Christian worship was still a family affair, a domestic type of gathering, a countercultural movement on the fringes of a decaying Roman culture. The dynamics of Christianity's encounter with the Greco-Roman world can best be seen by looking at the practice of Christian initiation as it developed during this significant period.

Baptism

Under the leadership of missionaries like Paul, the church had experienced dramatic growth. By the time of the Diocletian persecution (A.D. 303), there were as many as forty Christian basilicas in Rome with many thousands of members. And yet, this rapid increase in the number of Christians occurred not under circumstances of easy admission, cultural accommodation, and lax membership requirements. To the contrary, baptismal practice in this period shows the church carefully defining itself against its pagan environment. Our major source on early baptisms is the *Apostolic Tradition* (sections 16-23) of Hippolytus of Rome, written around A.D. 215. The *Apostolic Tradition* depicts baptism not as a momentary rite but, rather, as part of a long process of initiation into the Christian community.

First, there was rigorous examination of all those who sought admission. Idolaters, actors, circus performers and organizers, pimps, gladiators, harlots, astrologers, and magicians were rejected because of the immoral and pagan connotations of such amusements. Soldiers and high government officials were not admitted because of their subservience to the pagan state. Artists and teachers, being notorious dabblers in pagan myths and fables, were only hesitatingly accepted. Rather than opening her doors to all comers, the church carefully attempted to differentiate herself from what she considered to be an alien and hostile pagan world.

For those who were admitted as "hearers" *(catechumens)*, a three-year period of instruction, Old Testament readings, and worship followed. Catechumens could attend the first part of Sunday worship, the *synaxis*—or Service of the Word—but they were dismissed before the Lord's Supper itself. After three years, *catechumens* who had proved themselves by their knowledge of the faith and by their virtuous lives were admitted as "candidates" *(competentes)*. A few weeks before Easter, these candidates were given instruction in the gospel (which was reserved until these final stages) and daily exorcisms and were carefully examined.

When those are chosen who are to be set apart for baptism, their lives are to be examined. Have they lived honestly during the time they were catechumens? Have they honored the widows, visited the sick, done all sorts of good things? If those who sponsor them testify that they have done these things, let them hear the Gospel.

From the time that they are separated, let a hand be laid on them daily for exorcism. When the day approaches on which they are to be baptized, the bishop exorcises each one of them that he may know if he is pure. If any of them is not good or not pure, let him be put aside, for he did not hear the word in faith. . . . (20)[1]

On Thursday before Easter, the candidates bathed, then fasted on Friday and Saturday. On Saturday a final exorcism was performed by the bishop:

He shall bid them all to pray and bend the knee. And laying his hand on them, he shall exorcise every alien spirit that they flee from them and never return to them again. And when he has finished exorcising, he shall breathe in their faces, and when he has signed their foreheads, ears, and noses, he shall raise them up. (20)

The night was spent in vigil, reading, and instruction. On Easter, as the first light of day appeared on the horizon, a prayer was said over the baptismal waters which recalled the many connotations of water within salvation history: the waters of creation, the water of the grave, the Red Sea crossing, Moses and the water from the rock, the water of Naaman's immersion, the water in Mary's womb, the River Jordan, the living water promised to the woman at the well, the water from the side of Christ, and the waters of Paradise. "Living water" (flowing from a fountain or poured into a tank from above) was specified. A house church which was found in Dura-Europas (c. A.D. 232) has a special baptismal room with a boxlike pool resembling a tomb, recalling the death-life meanings of baptism which we mentioned in the previous chapter.

Two anointing oils, "the oil of thanksgiving" and the "oil of exorcism," were blessed. Candidates removed all clothing and jewelry (". . . let nothing alien go down into the water.") and renounced ". . . Satan, and all your servants, and all your works." The oil of exorcism was rubbed over each candidate by a deacon; then the deacon led the candidates into the water where individual baptizing was done by a presbyter (or bishop).

In the water the presbyter asked each candidate, "Do you believe in God, the Father Almighty?"

[1]*La Tradition Apostolique de saint Hippolyte Essai de reconstruction,* trans. Dom Bernard Botte (Münster Westfalen: Aschendorff Verlagsbuchhandlung, 1963). I have made an English translation of this material from the Latin which Botte has reconstructed. Subsequent references to this work will be identified by section number in the body of the chapter.

"I believe," responded the candidate. The presbyter then pushed the candidate under the water.

"Do you believe in Jesus Christ, the Son of God, who was born of the Holy Spirit from the virgin Mary, and was crucified under Pontius Pilate, and was dead and buried, and rose again the third day, and sat at the right hand of the Father, and will come to judge the living and the dead?"

"I believe."

The candidate was pushed under the water a second time, then asked, "Do you believe in the Holy Spirit, the holy church, and the resurrection of the flesh?"

"I believe."

For a third and final time the candidate went under the baptismal water. Our Apostles' Creed grew out of this early baptismal confessional formula.

Now each baptizand (i.e., person being baptized) was fully anointed with the oil of thanksgiving, clothed (possibly in a new white robe—"put on the garment of Christ"), led into the congregation, and presented to the bishop. The bishop then confirmed the baptism (the forerunner of the later separate rite of "confirmation") by a token repetition of the laying on of hands and anointing. The bishop made the sign of the cross upon the forehead of the newly baptized, kissed and greeted each baptizand with, "The Lord be with you."

"And with your spirit," responded each new Christian.

For the first time the newly baptized joined the faithful in their prayers, followed by the kiss of peace and the offertory, in which those baptized offered gifts of food. During the actual Communion, in addition to the usual bread and water mixed with wine, the newly baptized were given a cup of water (symbolizing inner baptism) and a cup of milk and honey, ". . . for the fulfillment of the promise which was made to the fathers when he spoke of a land flowing with milk and honey, in which way Christ gave also his flesh, by which those who believe are nourished like small children, the sweetness of the word making sweet bitterness of heart. . . ." (4)

Easter Eucharist followed with the bishop instructing the initiates in the meaning of each part. While this baptismal account in the *Apostolic Tradition* represents only the baptismal practices in Rome at this time, we can assume that here we have the basic form for Christian initiation in this early period of the church.

We should also note that Hippolytus describes the baptism of children from Christian families: "And they shall baptize the little children first. And if they can answer for themselves, let them answer. But if they cannot, let their parents answer or someone from their family" (4). By the third century the baptism of children was widely accepted by the church (Tertullian was among the few who objected to the practice); however, parents were also permitted to delay the baptism of their children. It is reasonable to assume that, even though the baptism of the children of Christian parents was a natural outgrowth of the early church's belief in the church as the family of God, care was given to see that baptized children were nurtured in the faith as they matured.

For those who experienced this lengthy period of training and these symbolically rich ceremonies of initiation and conversion, there must have been a feeling of having died to one's old self and having been born into a new life. In baptism, one was incorporated into the community of faith. Unlike the ceremonial washings of some of the pagan religions, Christian baptism was seen as a once-and-for-all action of a gracious God rather than a repeatable self-cleansing by a believer. As Tertullian noted, "Christians are made, not born." The Christian life required conversion, re-formation, and discipline on the part of the believer. Baptism was not some magical ablution. It required response on the part of the recipient and a new orientation of one's life. As Christ rose from the tomb on Easter as the resurrected Lord, so these initiates emerged from the baptismal waters as new and redeemed people. "Once you were no people but now you are God's people" (1 Peter 2:10a).

Eucharist

The end result of baptism, the high privilege for which it qualified one, was participation in the sacred meal of the congregation. After being baptized "into the name of Christ," one was able to eat and drink with Christ and his church at the Lord's Table.

By the beginning of the second century, the sacred meal of Christians was generally called "Eucharist" (meaning 'Thanksgiving"). The *Didache* (c. A.D. 100) instructs Christians, "On the Lord's Day meet and break bread and offer the Eucharist, after having first confessed your offenses, so that your sacrifice may be pure." Justin's *Apologia* (c. A.D. 150) describes worship in the church at Rome as a gathering on Sunday, led by a "president" (as yet there seems to be no status distinction between *cleros* and *laos*), which begins with readings from the apostles or the writings of the prophets "as long as time permits" followed by a sermon by the president "urgently admonishing his hearers to practice these beautiful teachings in their lives." "Then all stand up together and recite prayers." Then bread and wine mixed with water are brought, the president offers prayers of thanksgiving "as much as in him lies," and the people respond with, "Amen." The Eucharist is then eaten, and leftovers are gathered by the deacons to take to orphans, widows, and others who are not present. Note that the Eucharist is preceded by the *synaxis*, or Service of the Word, which closely parallels synagogue worship.

In the *Didache* and *Apologia* we have only sketches of a basic pattern for Sunday worship. There are as yet no full texts of prayers and, while the pattern seems to be fixed by this period, there appears to be much local variation and flexibility of content. The themes of the prayer were fixed, but the actual wording of the eucharistic prayer was the duty of the one who recited the prayer. By the third century, a clear shape for Sunday worship emerges, and for the first time we have the actual wording of the eucharistic prayer, the heart of the Eucharist. That prayer is found in section 4 of the *Apostolic Tradition*.

We have already noted the *Apostolic Tradition*'s account of Christian initiation. Hippolytus also gives us a description of a third-century Eucharist in the context of the ordination of a bishop. It would not be an exaggeration to say that, through the legacy of this detailed account of an early Eucharist, Hippolytus has become the most important figure in the history of the early liturgy and, as we shall see in later chapters, a source of liturgical innovation in our own day.

Because of the conservative purpose of the *Apostolic Tradition*—Hippolytus's attempt to record the "correct" rites and customs so that they would not be destroyed by "mindless innovators"—we are confident that we have before us a model for some of the earliest eucharistic practices in the Western church.

In the Hippolytan description of the Eucharist, a number of details strike us at first glance. As we noted before, only baptized and sufficiently instructed persons participate. The meal occurs as the usual climax of Sunday worship. After the Service of the Word, the deacons collect loaves of bread and jugs of wine and present them to the bishop who stands and presides at the table. The distinguishing characteristic of the Hippolytan eucharistic prayer is its brevity and simplicity. Behind the eucharistic liturgies of the Western church stands a long development in the course of which eucharistic prayers became loaded with secondary elements which obscured their structure and essential parts. Here we see all of the main parts which found their way, in this order (with a few exceptions), into all later eucharistic prayers. The parts of this prayer are set forth in a bold, straightforward manner.

First, an Introductory Dialogue (*Sursum corda*—"Lift up your hearts") was spoken (probably derived from synagogue practices) between the bishop and the people:

Bishop: The Lord be with you.

People: And with your Spirit.

Bishop: Lift up your hearts.

People: We have them with the Lord.

Bishop: Let us give thanks (*eucharistia*) to the Lord.

People: It is right and proper. (4)

The bishop then recites the eucharistic prayer. In the *Apostolic Tradition* we are given a model for a eucharistic prayer, not a fixed text. The presbyters, standing on each side of the bishop before the table, extend their hands over the offering. This is variously called the prayer of thanksgiving, anaphora (from the Greek, meaning "to offer up"), "Prayer of Consecration" (a misnomer from the Reformation), canon, or eucharistic prayer. We will separate the prayer into its various parts.

Thanksgiving

We give you thanks, O God, through your dear Child, Jesus Christ, whom you sent us in these last days to save us, redeem us, and inform us of your plan. He is your Word, inseparable from you, through whom you created all things and whom, being well pleased with him, you sent from heaven to a virgin's womb. He was conceived and took flesh and was manifested as your Son, born of the Holy Spirit and of the virgin. And he, accomplishing your will and acquiring a holy people for you, stretched out his hands as he suffered to free from suffering those who trust you. (4)

To comprehend the introductory thanksgiving section of the anaphora, we must be reminded that, among the Jews, the "blessing" of food is always a "thanksgiving." A Jew does not say, "Bless this food," but, rather, "Blessed be God who gave this food." "God is great; God is good; let us thank him for our food," is the essence of these table blessings. The Greek words *eucharistein* ("to give thanks") and *eulogein* ("to praise") are used without great distinction in the New Testament (see Mark 8:6-7). To give thanks to God is to praise God, to proclaim God's mighty deeds. The basis for our thanksgiving is gratitude before the great works of God. The opening, "Let us give thanks to the Lord," sets the tone for the prayer and for the entire Eucharist itself.

The basic form of the eucharistic prayer is modeled on Jewish "eucharistic" prayers, the *berekah*, in the Old Testament (2 Chronicles 6:4; Nehemiah 9:5f.; etc.) as well as the *kiddush* which is prayed over the cup of wine in the sacred meals of Judaism. The outline of these prayers is always the same: There is first a series of thanksgivings, often in the form of blessings of God for divine mercies in the past. These thanksgivings then are used to justify certain petitions, which are appended to the series of thanksgivings. In Hippolytus, the times of thanksgiving are four: the action of the Word of God in creation, the incarnation, the Passion, and at the Last Supper. The prayer of thanksgiving in Hippolytus is, therefore, best seen as a Christianized Jewish table blessing.

The content of the introductory section of the prayer corresponds directly to the Christological part of the Apostles' Creed and is itself a kind of summary of the core of apostolic teaching and preaching. Here we have a public proclamation of the deeds of God, a hymn of praise, making known and recalling to the eucharistic assembly what God has done.

The meaning of the vivid "he stretched out his hands" is undoubtedly an allusion to Isaiah 65:2 ("Each day I stretched out my hand to a rebellious people."). The phrase is repeated by Paul in Romans 10:21 as a powerful image of divine compassion on the cross. But note that in comparison to our later liturgies for the Mass and the Lord's Supper, there is surprisingly little emphasis on the Passion and suffering of Christ.

Narrative of Institution

When he was handed over to undergo voluntary suffering, to destroy death and to break the chains of the Devil, to crush hell beneath his feet, establish the rule [of faith], and manifest his resurrection, taking bread, he gave thanks to you and said: "Take, eat; this is my body broken for you." In the same way, taking the chalice, he said: "This is my blood which is shed for you. When you do this, do it in memory of me." (4)

The thundering words "to break the chains of the Devil, to crush hell beneath his feet, establish the rule [of faith], and manifest his resurrection . . ." represent more of a *Christus Victor* image of Christ's saving work rather than the narrow forensic and substitutionary atonement images that were to dominate later Christian theology.

The tone in Hippolytus is one of joyful triumph at the victory of Christ in the war of human liberation. It is an eschatological prayer, a future-oriented prayer which sings of a new age in which the whole cosmos is redeemed and all things are being made new. The chains which once bound humanity no longer enslave it. Here, in Hippolytus, there is no doubt that Christians are partaking of a resurrection meal, not a wake for a departed hero. This discovery has had profound implications for recent liturgical reform.

The words of institution are a simple and undeveloped free rendering of 1 Corinthians 11:23 into the indicative form. There is no special emphasis on the words, no attempt to highlight them. They merely come as an integral part of the entire salvation story. This is interesting, especially in the light of later developments which focused almost exclusively on the words of institution as the core of the eucharistic prayer to the exclusion of other aspects of Christ's saving work.

Anamnesis (Remembrance)

Remembering, then, his death and resurrection, we offer you this bread and cup, giving you thanks for judging us worthy to stand before you and serve you as priests. (4)

Immediately following the words of institution comes the so-called *anamnesis*. This is usually rendered in English as "remembrance." Gregory Dix suggested that this should be translated, not as something remembered from the past, but as a "re-representation" or "re-calling" of some past event, making it present.[2] To recall something in the liturgy, particularly for the Jews, is not to focus on the dead past; it is to proclaim its presently manifested power and our place within its present reality. The

[2] Gregory Dix, *The Shape of the Liturgy* (Westminster: Dacre Press, 1945), p. 245.

"remembering" which takes place here is therefore more accurately understood as "proclamation," "participation" (rather than mere historical recollection) of the type understood by the prayers of the Jewish Passover seder (chapter 1) in which those who later remembered the Exodus from Egypt were presently part of that saving work by the very act of their remembrance.

Epiclesis (Invocation)

Then follows the *epiclesis* which asks for a divine response to the church's offering in the preceding *anamnesis*. The spirit is invoked upon the offering and upon the participants. Unlike later developments in the Eastern church, the *epiclesis* does not ask for a change in the bread and wine into the body and blood—although this may be implied by the following invocation.

> And we ask you to send your Holy Spirit on the offering of the holy church. In gathering them together, grant to those who share in your holy mysteries so to take part that they may be filled with the Holy Spirit for the strengthening of their faith in truth. (4)

Doxology

> So that we may praise you and glorify you through your Child Jesus Christ, through whom be to you glory and honour with the Holy Spirit in holy church now and throughout all ages. Amen. (4)

The prayer of thanksgiving ends with a concluding doxology, reinforcing the eucharistic nature of this prayer as a hymn of praise in response to human liberation in Christ. The final "Amen" of the people signifies their assent and participation in all that has gone before. The faithful then move toward the table and receive the eucharistic bread and wine. After the meal, the deacons gather leftovers for the poor, and the faithful depart into a hostile world in which many of them may pay a high price for their faith.

They will gladly pay the price because in baptism they are new people and in the Eucharist they have had both a foretaste and an enactment of a joy that is worth all cost.

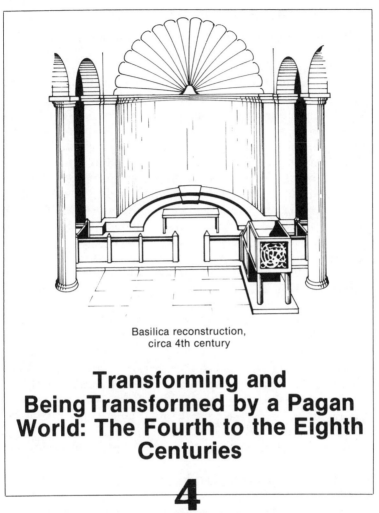

Basilica reconstruction,
circa 4th century

Transforming and BeingTransformed by a Pagan World: The Fourth to the Eighth Centuries

4

In A.D. 313 the emperor Constantine made "peace" with the church, and Christianity became respectable, developing under the benevolent eyes of the Roman Empire. In the next few centuries, Christian worship not only transformed paganism but also, like the church's life as a whole, was transformed in the process. The church never exists in a vacuum. Those who convert to the faith come with a cultural heritage which the cleansing water of baptism never fully eradicates. Christian worship assimilated the cultural heritage of the Greco-Roman world—architecture, art, dress, civic affairs, ceremonial, language, and philosophy—and with this assimilation changed in some fundamental ways.

Architecture for Worship

Constantine and his family promoted Christianity as the new state religion, erecting magnificent buildings for worship in Rome, Constantinople, and Jerusalem. The new crowds who were being converted to the faith needed larger houses of worship. Christian worship, no longer a domestic sort of gathering in a house church, was becoming "public worship"; and the new public buildings, which more appropriately expressed Christianity's new status, greatly influenced the liturgy. The basilica, a Roman public building, was adopted as the primary architectural form for Christian worship. Basilicas, among the Romans' most impressive buildings, were meeting halls where people gathered for law courts, markets, and important governmental functions. Because of the building's associations with dignity, power, and prestige, it is natural that the basilica should have been chosen for housing Christian worship.

The plan of a Christian basilica was simple—a wide, central aisle bordered by columns and side aisles, with an apse opposite the main entrance. The apse contained a *cathedra*, or bishop's chair, around which were seats for other clergy. Seated at his *cathedra* (Roman philosophers gave their instruction while seated), the bishop led the services and preached. In front of the apse, closer to the assembled people was a small, square table which, in churches like Saint Peter's in Rome, was given prominence by being placed under a canopylike *ciborium*. Scripture was read from a pulpitlike *ambo*.

The exterior of the basilica was given little attention or decoration. The interior was the glory of the building, usually covered with mosaics or paintings of Christian scenes. When one entered the church, one left the old familiar world for the strange new world of faith. Upon entering the dim interior of a basilica, one's eyes were led down a long, columned vista to the table and *cathedra*. In such a building the actions of the liturgy and its leaders were obviously "up there," at the end of the building, under the apse. The interior was simple, dramatic, and linear, a fitting space for processions, pomp, and drama which gave the liturgy a new imperial sense of dignity and ceremoniousness which pervaded Christian worship centuries thereafter.

Martyria

Other pagan buildings were often adapted by Christians. Roman mausoleums, built in round, square, octagonal, or cruciform plans, were adapted as Christian *martyria* to house the tombs of saints and martyrs. The church assembled at the *martyria* to celebrate the anniversary of the death of a martyr—the martyr's "birthday into eternity," as they called it. In Jerusalem, a large, round, domed *martyrium* was erected on the traditional site of Jesus' resurrection. These great buildings contributed to the steadily growing practice of veneration of the martyrs. Roman mausoleums also provided the architectural form for many early baptistries. The baptistries housed a central pool which often resembled a tomb or sarcophagus, giving visible form to the death-resurrection associations of baptism. The Roman mausoleum, with its centrally oriented space, was ideal for buildings which were built to focus on one object or activity. In the East, these round, octagonal, and cruciform buildings were widely used for churches, giving Eastern worship a different orientation from that in the West. The Western church eventually came to view the linear, rectangular basilican plan as the only appropriate architectural arrangement for worship, a development which helped to determine the focus and form of the liturgy.

Pagan Gifts

Other aspects of pagan culture influenced Christian worship during the premedieval period. While musical instruments were excluded from Christian worship because of their former noisy use to entice the gods to pagan sacrifices, plain homophonic singing, simple melodies, and responsively chanted psalms were regularly employed. Just as the church adopted pagan architectural forms for new church buildings, it also used pagan artistic motifs and symbols for interior decoration, liturgical utensils, and tombs. A familiar pagan artistic theme, Orpheus, became the prototype for "Christ, the Good Shepherd," one of the most popular early artistic representations of Christ. Doves, peacocks, sheep, fishermen, wine pressers, even Amor and Psyche were "baptized" and enlisted in the service of visual representation of the faith.

The fourth-century transition from Greek to Latin liturgical language gave a new style to Christian prayer. The conciseness, clarity, and straightforward simplicity of Latin as well as the

Roman proclivity for forensic images greatly influenced the texts of Sunday worship. Terms such as "sacrifice," "oblation," and "redemption," while they were all parts of the Christian heritage, appeared with increasing frequency and emphasis. Older, more flexible worship patterns gave way to more formalism and greater fixity of liturgical texts. Church orders, like that of Hippolytus, were replaced with books (sacramentaries) which contained fixed prayers to be read by worship leaders.

The ceremonies of the imperial court influenced Christian rites. Bishops, now elevated to prestigious positions of leadership in the empire, were granted special privileges. Fellow clerics now bowed to bishops as they sat on their *cathedras* as Romans had bowed to secular judges and consuls who sat upon their seats of honor. Attendants followed the bishop as he led the liturgy in the same way that attendants followed state officials in the old court ceremonials. Processions, torches, lights, and incense—familiar customs of imperial court ceremonial—were introduced into the church's worship. Processional crosses and bishop's crosiers (an imperial staff which later came to be interpreted as a shepherd's crook), candlesticks (first used simply for illumination and later given theological rationale), and incense (both a mysterious symbol of the divine and a cover for foul odors) entered Christian worship after the fourth century. The new adornments absorbed scriptural and allegorical meanings. In the liturgy, functional and aesthetic considerations usually come first; theological justification comes later.

The kiss (an intimate greeting and a sign of veneration of holy objects in the ancient world) was adopted by Christians. Altars, books, newly baptized persons, and fellow Christians (kissed before the offering in the Eucharist with the "kiss of peace") were kissed in worship.

The street clothing of the middle class of the day continued to be worn by conservative clergy after it had passed out of fashion. What was once everyday dress became sacred vestment. The alb was basic street attire; the amice, a collar; the maniple, a handkerchief or napkin; the chasuble, a type of coat. The clerical stole, a rather controversial article of clothing at first (because of the debate over the growing separation of clergy and laity), was formerly a badge of civil office in the Roman state. All of these adopted elements, associated originally with the ceremonies and trappings of the imperial court, gave the liturgy a growing sense of drama and majesty and the clergy a growing sense of separation from the laity. Another pagan gift to Christian worship was the custom of facing toward the east for prayer. The practice was given theological rationale by the east being the direction of Christ's ascension and Second Coming. Church buildings were often oriented *ad lucem*, i.e., with the facade of the building facing the sun's eastward rising. Pagans sometimes built their temples in this manner. This eastward orientation had the disadvantage of forcing the congregation to turn away from the table and face the front door in order to pray in the eastward position. The celebrant was at no inconvenience since he faced east across the table. Eventually churches were built with the apse facing east so that people and priest could face in the same direction, like one great eastward moving procession. This new building orientation meant that the celebrant no longer faced the congregation during the liturgy and began facing the wall of the apse (or the altar, a place of priestly sacrifice, which had replaced the older eucharistic table) with his back to the congregation—a significant change with important implications for the liturgy.

Theological Disputes

Along with the influences of paganism and Greco-Roman culture, the heated fourth-century theological controversies significantly modified the liturgy. Arius touched off a great debate over the Godhead. Against older Trinitarian Christological formulae, he affirmed the absolute uniqueness and transcendence of God and the corresponding subordination of the Son. Arius's "subordinationism" contended that the Son, created *ex nihilo* by the Father, cannot fully know nor be equal to the Father. The Council of Nicaea, in an attempt to restore political and theological order in the empire, condemned Arianism in A.D. 325. The Son is "begotten, not made," Nicaea claimed. The son is mediator of humanity to God the Father because the Son is equal to the Father. At stake here is the question "To whom are Christians to address their prayers?" Most early Christian liturgical prayers addressed God the Father. Nicaea through its rather belabored creedal formulation, in order to preserve the equality of Christ, affirmed the Son's worthiness to be the focus of prayer because of his status as divine mediator. We pray to God through *Christ.*

There were other disputes: Donatist (a debate over what constituted a valid ordination), Pelagian (an argument over original sin), and Nestorian (a debate over the relationship of the human and divine natures in the Christ), which along with the Arian controversy were to affect liturgy and liturgical theology. It was a time of theological entrenchment and attempts to impose order on a rather disordered church. Heresy inevitably bred overreaction against the heresy. The result of most of the controversies was a stronger emphasis upon the divinity of Christ at the expense of the priestly mediatorial role of the man Christ Jesus which had been part of New Testament Christology (John 16:23; Hebrews 4:14; etc.). In stressing the divinity of Christ and the majesty of the Son of God, Christendom lost the earlier Christological equilibrium. The Eucharist, the Supper of the Lord, was gradually transformed, like the church's Christology, into something of awe, mystery, and distance. Chrysostom, preaching to his congregation, spoke of the Eucharist as the "shuddering hour" and the "terrible and awful table." The people began to step back in awe and wonder from the once accessible table. Heresy had been defeated—at some cost to the liturgy.

Baptism

The church's new relationship with the world and the theological disputes had a noticeable effect on the rites of initiation. The sheer size of the church and the large numbers of new converts made older initiation practices impractical. By the fourth century, rites and instructions for initiation had been compressed into a period of a few weeks. Although adult baptism was still the norm, small children were increasingly brought for baptism, their baptismal response made vicariously by their parents or sponsors. Baptism was still associated with the Easter vigil. Symbolic additions to the rite, such as the giving of salt ("You are the salt of the earth") and a candle ("You are the light of the world") to the candidates, were made at this time. In some localities baptismal water was sometimes sprinkled toward the congregation as a reminder or renewal of baptism.

In this century confirmation is first mentioned as a separate part of Christian initiation. The separation of confirmation from the baptismal rite probably began when persons who had been baptized by a heretical bishop or who had lapsed from the faith and wished to be restored were publicly received by a laying on of hands. Confirmation is also used for the first time to refer to one's first reception of the Eucharist as a sign of the completion of one's initiation. With a larger number of initiates, the practice arose in Rome of baptism by the local presbyter, with later laying on of hands or confirmation by the bishop whenever he was available. The fragmentation of Christian initiation into two separate rites, baptism and confirmation, had begun.

The Donatist controversy gave a new definition of what constitutes a valid baptism—water and the Word. The Pelagian controversy led to an increased emphasis upon original sin and its eradication by baptism. Emphasis on baptism as the cleansing of human sinfulness eventually led to an increase in clinical or deathbed baptisms and infant baptisms. Baptism was declining as a multifaceted experience of Christian initiation. It was becoming a rite of childbirth rather than a rite of initiation, a method of eradicating an individual's original sin, a sign of an individual's birth into a Christian culture rather than an incorporation into a separated community of faith.

Eucharist

The Eucharist continued to be the central act of Sunday worship. (Constantine proclaimed Sunday a day of rest in A.D. 321.) Despite much local variation in the form of the Eucharist, in the West two main families of Latin liturgies emerged—the *Gallic* and the *Roman*. Gallic rites were generally those liturgies practiced in churches around Milan and north of the Alps. Among the notable characteristics of Gallic rites were a high degree of congregational participation; elaborate, dramatic, symbolically rich ceremonials; and poetic, florid, exhortatory prayers. Under Charlemagne, there emerged a program to suppress the Gallic rite in order to bring more uniformity of practices by imposition of the Roman rite. Through a long series of compromises, additions, and deletions, the end result was a "Gallicanization" of the Roman rite.

The Roman family of rites included those liturgies used in Rome and North Africa. Typical of the Roman mind, Roman rites tended to be terse, simple, orderly, and sombre. There was little popular hymnody or spoken congregational response. After the eighth century, the Roman rite gradually superseded other rites in the Western church.

What happened to the Eucharist itself between the seventh and eighth centuries is clear in an examination of the two rites. By the seventh century, Gallic liturgy had the form delineated in the next section.

Gallic Rites

The Fore Mass (as the Service of the Word was now being called) began with a sung antiphon which accompanied the entrance of the clergy. The bishop greeted the people with, "The Lord is always with you," to which they responded, "And with your spirit." Three songs were then sung: the *Trisagion* ("Holy, holy, holy. . . ."), the *Kyrie Eleison* ("Lord, have mercy. . . ."), and the *Benedictus* (Luke 1:68-79). These were followed by the bishop's prayer, which often alluded to the particular festival or season.

The lessons were then read: Old Testament and one of the epistles (or Acts), preceded or followed by *Benedictus es* and a responsorial chant. Prior to the Gospel lesson, the Gospel book was brought forward in a procession which was led by seven torchbearers while (in some instances) the *Trisagion* was chanted. "Glory be to you, O Lord," the people responded when the Gospel was announced. The *Trisagion* was chanted again after the Gospel reading, and a sermon was given by the bishop or a priest. A prayer for the church, in the form of a litany, followed the sermon; each petition was offered by a deacon, with the people responding, "Lord, have mercy." A concluding collect by the bishop summed up the prayer. Any catechumens were then dismissed by a deacon.

The Eucharist itself began with the offering of bread and wine, given by the people and brought forward in solemn procession as songs of praise were chanted. A preface (setting forth the special reasons for celebrating the day) and a variable prayer (varying according to the time of the year) followed. The diptychs were read (i.e., the names of those who had made the offering and the names of the dead for whom prayers were requested). The peace was then passed (note its position here some time after the offering), accompanied by the hymns and followed by a variable prayer. The eucharistic prayer then followed, with major portions of the prayer varying according to the day. The *Sursum corda* ("Lift up your hearts. . . ."), followed by the *Sanctus* and a variable prayer, led to the words of institution. Another variable prayer closed the eucharistic prayer. The *anamnesis*, oblation, *epiclesis*, and prayer for the communicants (which we remember from their place in the Roman eucharistic prayer of Hippolytus) were no longer always present. The large portions of variable prayers and prefaces tended to overshadow some of the basic older elements of the eucharistic prayer and to clutter the prayer with many variable additions and nonessential elements which changed from Sunday to Sunday.

Roman Rites

While we have no surviving text of the Roman rite between Hippolytus and the sacramentaries of the seventh century, we can see in later texts the many changes that occurred during this period. By the time of Pope Leo the Great (440-461), "Mass" was the name by which the Eucharist was known. The term comes from the "dismissal" at the end of the liturgy (*Ite missa est*—"You are dismissed"). A fifth-century Mass must have looked something like this: An introit psalm began the Mass as the clergy entered (choirs and more elaborate music were beginning to be used). Following the Kyries, a variable collect was offered by the celebrant (collects being short, concise prayers following the typical form of [1] address to God, [2] citing of a divine attribute by which a petition is being made, [3] petition, [4] reason for making the petition, and [5] a doxology). Then the lections were read, interspersed by chanted psalms. The people presented gifts of bread and wine at the offertory as the choir sang another psalm. Then another collect was prayed over the offering *(super oblata)*.

The ancient introductory dialogue and *Sursum corda*, ending with the singing of the *Sanctus*, led into the eucharistic prayer which is now called the "canon." This prayer contains the old elements of the words of institution and *anamnesis* with a new emphasis on oblation with a petition that this oblation might be taken by "your angels to your altar on high." Note the absence of an *epiclesis*, or prayer for the communicants, and the general lack of emphasis on *eucharistia* in the canon:

> Make for us right, spiritual, worthy this oblation, which is the figure of the body and blood of our Lord Jesus Christ, who the day before he suffered, took bread into his holy hands, looked up to heaven, to you, holy Father, almighty, eternal God; giving thanks, he blessed, broke,

and having broken, gave it to his apostles and disciples, saying, Take and eat of this, all of you, for this is my body which shall be broken for many. In the same way, after supper, on the day before he suffered, he took the cup, looked up to heaven to you, holy Father, almighty, eternal God; giving thanks, he blessed, and gave it to his apostles and disciples, saying, Take and drink of this, all of you, for this is my blood. As often as you do this, you make memorial of me, until I come again. Therefore, calling to mind his glorious passion, resurrection from the dead, and ascension into heaven, we offer you this immaculate sacrifice, this reasonable sacrifice, this bloodless sacrifice, this holy bread and cup of eternal life, and we pray and beseech you to take up this offering by the hands of your angels to your altar on high, as you deigned to receive the gifts of our just servant Abel and the sacrifice of our father Abraham, and that offered to you by Melchisedech the high priest.[1]

While the idea of sacrifice, Christ's and ours, had long been associated with the Eucharist, this prayer gives extraordinary prominence to the idea of the Mass as a priestly sacrifice and reflects the Western church's emphasis on Christ's words of institution (rather than the Eastern church's emphasis on the *epiclesis*) as the focus of the eucharistic action.

Gregory the Great (590-604) sought to abridge the gradually enlarged and rather unwieldy Roman rite. But in the process of Gregorian revisions, prayers of intercession were absorbed into the canon, adding to its complexity and diminishing its unity. The rise of the cult of martyrs and saints also intruded into the liturgy with long lists of saints read during the Mass and numerous variable prefaces and prayers which changed according to specific saints' days. This focus upon the saints during the Mass tended to accentuate the works of the saints and obscure the central saving work of Christ. The Lord's Prayer was placed at the end of the canon as a kind of extended Amen. During this period a gospel procession with incense and candles came into being, the Scripture lessons were generally reduced to two, and preaching became infrequent. The rise of Mariology added frequent references to Mary to the text of the Mass. The peace was moved from its traditional location with the offertory and placed between the fraction (breaking of bread) and Communion.

---

[1] Marion J. Hatchett, "Seven Pre-Reformation Eucharistic Liturgies: Historic Rites Arranged for Contemporary Celebration," *The St. Luke's Journal of Theology*, vol. XVI, no. 3 (June, 1973), pp. 50-51. © The School of Theology, The University of the South, Sewanee, TN 37375. Used by permission.

The end result of all this was that the Roman canon lost the brevity, the sense of orderly progression in its eucharistic prayers and actions, and the sense of joyful thanksgiving which the earlier Roman Eucharist of Hippolytus displayed. A richness and sense of drama now infused the rites at the expense of the older clarity and unity. The Mass had been transformed from a communal eucharistic act into a solemn priestly sacrifice, a sacred pageant with less congregational participation. The people were less active participants and more passive spectators.

As this significant period ended, a number of new practices were begun which were to have lasting consequences for the liturgy. Gregory is credited with the invention of the *schola cantorum* ("school of singers") which introduced into the liturgy new, embellished and antiphonal hymns which varied according to the changing seasons of the church year. While the *schola cantorum* and its music added beauty to certain rather "business-like" parts of the service (entrance of the clergy, offertory, and the people's Communion), it also meant difficult, more elaborate music which the laity were less likely to sing. It, therefore, signaled another step in clerical monopolization of the people's responses and acclamations in worship.

Fifth-century sacramentaries had included a number of collects for masses on various occasions: a wedding or anniversary, illness, epidemic, for good weather, and for the dead. From these early prayers for someone or some good cause came the development of entire masses which were offered for various people or causes—the "votive Mass." From the seventh century on, ordained monks and priests were frequently endowed by some wealthy donor to "say Mass," often several times a day, often with no one even present except the celebrant himself. The addition of intercessions into the prayers of the Mass had led to the practice of entire masses becoming intercessory. Despite numerous contemporary cautions against this multiplication of masses and private votive celebrations throughout the week, the votive Mass eventually became the dominant type of Latin Mass. Saint Peter Damian, expressing shock at the abuse of votive masses by an often ignorant clergy, complained that Christ's sacrifice for the whole world had now been reduced to "the benefit of one limited individual."

Was this a time of development or decline? There is no doubt that Christianity emerged from this period as a very different kind of faith. The fourth-century theological disputes were solved in somewhat unsatisfactory ways. Christendom was divided into East and West. And Christian worship was to lose much of its old vitality even as it gained a new richness. Worship practices were begun which eventually had tragic consequences. The Jesuit scholar Josef Jungmann gives us what is perhaps our most optimistic assessment of this period before the Middle Ages:

> The life of the Church can be regarded as a continuation of the Incarnation: new men, new nations, new cultures are constantly being taken up by the Church and built into the Mystical Body of Christ. These, in turn, determine to a certain extent the particular forms which the Church's life assumes. The process exemplifies the famous principle: Grace supposes nature; grace does not destroy but perfects nature. . . . Liturgy supposes culture, which it does not destroy but rather perfects.[2]

[2] Josef A. Jungmann, *The Early Liturgy to the Time of Gregory the Great* (Notre Dame, Ind.: University of Notre Dame Press, 1959), pp. 164-165.

High altar,
Gloucester Cathedral

Elaboration and Fragmentation: The Middle Ages

5

We now know that the Middle Ages were not the "Dark Ages." The foundations of the modern Western World were laid during this lively period. It is here that modern political democracy, capitalism, urbanism, science, and medicine had their beginnings. The great Gothic cathedrals are testimony to this age as the Age of Faith, a time when the church not only succeeded in making peace with its world but also, in a great sense, succeeded in conquering its world. But in the worship of the church, while the medieval period was a time of dramatic development of the liturgy, much of that development is now considered to be decline. The decline centers upon the central liturgical fact of this period—the dissolution of the worshiping community.

From the sixth century onward, the altar (the once freestanding table) was placed with increasing frequency against the apsidal wall of the church. No longer could the celebrant stand behind the altar and face the people. From the year 1000, the priest normally celebrated Mass with his back to the congregation. At about the same time, altars acquired a retable (a shelf or ledge behind the altar) upon which were placed candles and, by the thirteenth century, a small cross. The altar was cluttered with books, ornaments, candles, and vessels so that it more closely resembled an elaborate sideboard rather than a table. The table had become an elevated altar before which stood a priest doing priestly activity as the congregation watched. This arrangement of and action before the altar shifted the central focus of the eucharistic action and signified a fundamental reinterpretation of the rite.

Monastic Influence

Monasticism, which flowered during this period, was to have a profound and mostly undesirable effect upon Sunday worship when monastic worship practices filtered into parish churches. A major contribution of monastic worship to parish worship was the Divine Office. The Divine Office is a noneucharistic service whose roots lie within the early *synaxis,* or Service of the Word (see chapter 2), which was ultimately derived from the synagogue. In the monasteries, monks sought to follow Paul's exhortation to "pray without ceasing" by weekly recitation of the entire Psalter at a series of daily services. The Divine Office was a noneucharistic prayer and Scripture service, usually without sermon, which was suited to the spiritual needs of a monastic community. Gradually, this monastic concept of daily, continuous, corporate prayer was imported into so-called secular churches. The prayer offices were often sung by groups of monks attached to the churches. Sometimes lay people and parish clergy attended these services to pray with the monks—mostly to listen to the monks' beautiful singing. By the eighth century, parish priests began reciting a private form of the daily prayer services by using the Breviary, a book which contained the daily offices for personal recitation. The use of this tended to keep the laity from active participation and fostered a noneucharistic, passive, individualized worship.

The earliest monasteries were lay communities. Benedict had discouraged and carefully regulated clerical members of his monasteries due to the difficulties of assimilating a practicing priest into an essentially lay community. But by the eighth century, as monasteries became more involved in missionary work, priests were admitted to the orders in great numbers. These priest-monks naturally wished to celebrate the Mass, a duty of their office. This meant that there were often more priests to celebrate than monks to participate. A number of priests often celebrated a number of masses on any given day within many monasteries, often without the presence of a worshiping community. The priest simply recited the text of the rite to himself. By the ninth century this new form of the Eucharist, which had arisen in response to the particular needs of the monasteries, was gradually being adopted by parish priests outside the monasteries. While a number of contemporary church leaders protested the multiplication of weekday masses and the increase in these private masses, the daily private Mass was becoming a widespread practice.

From these daily private masses evolved what came to be known as the "Low Mass," a subdued, rather mechanical service "said" by a priest with his back to whatever people might be present, without music, spoken in a language (Latin) which the people no longer understood. In fact, the canon of the Mass (formerly the eucharistic prayer, or prayer of thanksgiving) was now said silently by the priest, an act of priestly devotion and respect which made the presence of the people utterly superfluous.

The Low Mass was compatible with the increasingly widespread notion that the more often one utilized the "means of grace" of the church, particularly by saying a mass or arranging for a mass to be said, the more one assured one's personal salvation and the salvation of the dead. In many of the monasteries and larger churches, wealthy donors endowed a chapel or "chantry" where priests were required daily to sing or say a mass for the souls of the donors. It was not uncommon for a large church or cathedral to have a dozen of these side chapels, each with its own altar, so that a score of masses were being said at the same time in the same church. The belief that merely saying a mass was, in itself, a work of righteousness was another factor which contributed to the proliferation of masses and thereby increased the fragmentation of the once unified Sunday Mass into a proliferation of daily masses.

Spoken inaudibly, in a language which was unintelligible to the average person, devoid of offertory procession or sermon or congregational music, the Low Mass reinforced the growing popular impression that the Mass is mostly a mechanical, priestly, individualistic affair which the priest said rather than the people acted, which is something to be watched rather than participated in by the people.

The ancient offertory procession, which had been a high point of early liturgies, gradually dropped out of the Mass. Originally, the offertory was a beautiful symbol of the oblation or the offering of the people and their gifts before God. It had long been the custom for the people to bring forward bread and wine and present them (along with other foodstuffs, oil, and wax) at the table. These gifts helped support the clergy, were used in the Eucharist, aided the charitable work of the congregation, and served as a ritualized way of claiming the people and the people's gifts as an integral part of the eucharistic action. "You not only lay your gift upon the altar; you lay *yourself* there as well," Augustine told his congregation as they made their offering.

In the Low Mass, there was often no one but the priest to make the offering; so no real offering could be made. The offertory became a time for the priest to prepare the bread and wine rather than for the people to offer the bread and wine. The offertory had grown in importance since the early controversies with the Gnostics when the offertory was emphasized as a sign of the goodness of creation and the worthiness of humanity to offer material things to God. But now, the liturgical thought of the day tended to stress the Mass as a mysterious, divine gift of God, through the church and its priests, given to the people rather than an offering of the people to God. With the deemphasis of the offertory procession, the clericalization of the Mass was complete. As the priest recited the prayers for the living in the canon, the words "Remember your servants who offer to you" became "Remember your servants *for whom we offer* or who offer to you" (italics mine). The Mass was now viewed as a priestly act in which even the people's presence—much less their active participation, offering, and Communion—was unnecessary.

Transubstantiation

The church had always assumed that Christ was present

whenever it celebrated the Eucharist. The church simply affirmed this presence, basing its affirmation upon Christ's promises and upon its own experience of his presence, without speculating on when or how or where Christ was present in the meal. Beginning in the fourth century, there was growing interest in *when* Christ was present, with increased speculation about "the moment of consecration."

In the early eucharistic prayer of Hippolytus, which we examined in chapter 3, we noted that the entire eucharistic prayer was a thankful proclamation or remembering of the full saving work and words of Christ. But as we move into the Middle Ages, the essential structure of the eucharistic prayer became more elaborate and loaded with secondary, esoteric elements. It was less evident that the eucharistic prayer was a proclamation of God's full saving work in Christ. It now had more the character of a petition, a formula to be repeated over the table in order to effect something in the rite. While this emphasis is not absent from the earliest eucharistic prayers, it was accentuated during the medieval period by the definition of a "moment of consecration." This moment, when the presence of Christ was felt to be especially real, when the canon reached its climax, came to be defined as that moment when the priest repeated the words, *"Hoc est corpus meum"* (*"This is my body"*). This had the effect of reducing the importance of the canon to a core of a few words which, at the moment when they were repeated by the priest, confected some mysterious reality in the elements of the meal. In settling upon these words of institution, the church reinforced the image of the priest as confector of the Mass rather than celebrant of the community's worship and, by elevating the words of the upper room, added to the growing identification of the Mass with only the Passion and crucifixion of Christ.

Having defined *when* Christ was present, by the ninth century the Western church had become concerned with questions of *how* Christ was present in the bread and wine. About 831, a monk named Paschasius Radbertus suggested that the body of Christ was present in the Mass by virtue of a miraculous transformation of the elements. While the outward appearance of the bread is unchanged, the original substance of the bread is transformed into the substance of the body of Christ. A fellow monk, Ratramnus, disputed Radbertus's idea of a miraculous change at the moment of consecration, and the doctrine was debated for many years. But the future was with Radbertus. At the Fourth Lateran Council in 1215, the doctrine of transubstantiation, as it had come to be called, became dogma.

The doctrine of transubstantiation can be accredited to the medieval mind's penchant for understanding and explaining everything in minute, scholastic detail, even something so inexplicable as the mystery of Christ's presence within Christian worship. The doctrine was based upon the predominant medieval philosophy of realism which separates reality into (1) "substances," which are the most real aspect of reality and participate in the universal "Ideas" which are the source of all reality, and (2) "accidents," which are the characteristics which we perceive in things: size, shape, weight, color. These "accidents," while they are connected to the substance of things, are not the essence of those things. In transubstantiation, the substance of bread is transformed, "transubstantiated," into the substance of the body of Christ. The "accidents" of the bread may make the bread appear to be ordinary bread to our senses, but its substance has been miraculously altered. Thus, the doctrine of transubstantiation, far from being a superstitious or simple-minded concept, is a sophisticated philosophical attempt to explain the real presence of Christ in terms of the reigning philosophy of that day.

But the doctrine's subtleties and sophistication were always part of its problem. From the beginning, the less sophisticated among the faithful fell into the notion that "the bread becomes the body of Christ"—presumably by some baffling magical process which is set in motion by the words of the priest. The most troubling aspect of the doctrine, as far as the later Protestant reformers were concerned, was that it tended to conflict with the church's historic belief that the Person of Christ unites his human and divine natures. According to transubstantiation, the substance of both Christ's human nature as well as his divine nature must be present in the consecrated bread and wine. In 1059, after getting into trouble for doubting the substantial change of the elements into the natural body and blood of Christ, Beranger of Tours was forced to sign a statement that, at the Mass, the priest actually touched the body of Christ and that the communicants "bit into the Lord's body with their teeth."

The final solidifying and sanctioning of the doctrine of

transubstantiation in 1215 had a detrimental effect upon Christian worship. The doctrine made the reception of the sacrament even more solemn and awe-full. During the Middle Ages, the cup was taken from the people. The laity now communed, when they dared to come forward and commune, only in the bread.

The bread itself had also changed. There is every reason to believe that the first Christian Eucharists used regular leavened bread. Later, as the Mass became more mysterious and sanctified, and more exclusively identified with the Jewish Passover, "special" unleavened bread was created. As the Christian priesthood became more closely identified with the Old Testament levitical priesthood, in the tenth and eleventh centuries the old levitical regulations for ritual bread (Leviticus 2:1-16; 6:14-23) were adopted. Ordinary table bread, the bread of the people, became unacceptable for the Mass. Priestly, "holy" bread was called for. The bread was no longer a sign of the offering of the stuff of everyday life; it became a pure white wafer, specially baked by sanctified hands, a sign of a pure and incorruptible priestly sacrifice.

In this climate of adoration and awe, it is understandable why the number of lay people who actually came forward to commune at the Mass declined. The decline of lay Communions had begun in the fifth century, but the doctrine of transubstantiation and the popular ideas about the doctrine made the laity even more reluctant to approach so great a mystery. The same Lateran Council which had officially decreed transubstantiation also had to decree that every Christian ought to receive the Eucharist at least once a year. But noncommunicating attendance at Mass remained the norm for Roman Catholics until the reforms of Pius X in the early twentieth century.

Of course, it would be unfair to say that the people who were present at a mass were unable to worship. The people were encouraged to pray their own prayers and to adore Christ's presence in the sacrament. Strong devotion to the person of Christ, continual reflection upon the suffering of Christ in his Passion, and adoration of the Blessed Sacrament became the core of late medieval piety. Genuflection, the rosary (prayer beads), and individual prayer books were created to keep the laity engaged in activity during the services. But it was activity which was personal, private, subjective, and individualized rather than corporate activity which was integrally related to the words and actions of the Mass itself. For the average faithful Christian, devotions outside of the Mass became the center of his or her piety. Within the Mass, the elevation of the host by the priest, accompanied by the ringing of a bell, became the main focus of popular devotion. The performing of the Mass was viewed as the way to produce the real presence of Christ so that Christ's people might adore him rather than commune with him.

The cult of the saints, which was now a major facet of Christian piety, contributed to the fragmentation of Sunday worship and the church year and added to the rise of devotions outside of Sunday worship. The popularity of the saints was probably related to the increasing distance between Christ and the Christian, a distance which, as we noted in the previous chapter, began in the Christological disputes of the fourth century. The growing importance of the saints, not to mention the ever-increasing devotion to Mary, and their inclusion in the church's worship tended to obscure the central focus of the liturgy and to fragment corporate worship into a score of minor celebrations and commemorations for the favorite saints and Mary. Often, when a saint's day fell on Sunday, commemoration of the saint over-shadowed the eucharistic celebration of Christ. The church year, once centered upon Easter as the highlight of the liturgy and the liturgical year, now became a cluttered calendar full of saints' days and celebrations of various doctrines rather than an orderly movement toward the central celebration of the atonement.

Baptism

Infant baptism had now become the normal practice in the West. At the beginning of the rite, the sign of the cross was made upon the child's breast and forehead, salt was placed upon the child's mouth, and then hands were laid upon his head. This was all that remained of the once lengthy preparatory catechumenate which we described in chapter 3. Baptism ceremonial had become quite elaborate and somewhat diffused, full of rich images, symbolic acts, anointings, and prayers. A beautiful blessing of the water was said over the font, recalling many of the biblical images of water and consecrating the water. Baptismal rubrics stated that once this blessing had been spoken by a priest, a baptized person who touched the water was, in effect, rebaptized. Thus, the objectification of the elements in the Mass was paralleled by a similar, almost magical objectification of the power of the water of baptism, apart from the total action of the church in administering the water and the response of the baptizand to the water.

A fear of limbo—a place for the souls of unbaptized infants who died—caused baptism to precede any catechetical instruction and to lose its former connection with the Easter vigil. Priests were to instruct their people on how to perform emergency baptisms in case of the impending death of an unbaptized infant. The wide variety of older baptismal imagery was overshadowed by the now central image of baptism as a bath to wash away the taint of original sin. Baptism was no longer a time for repentance, confession of faith, the gift of the Holy Spirit, death and resurrection, and conversion into the community; it was mostly a time for an individual's sin to be removed so that his or her soul would be fit for eternity. Godparents were urged to teach the baptized child the Apostles' Creed, the Ave Maria, the Lord's Prayer, how to genuflect, and to see that the child was confirmed "as soon as the bishop comes within a distance of seven miles."

Confirmation had now emerged as a separate rite which was usually performed sometime well after baptism, in early adolescence, and involved the imposition of hands with a prayer for the gift of the "sevenfold Spirit." This development marked the final dissolution of the once-unified rite of Christian initiation and tended to disjoin the gift of the Holy Spirit from baptism. Medieval theologians labored to explain this new rite. Aquinas spoke of confirmation as "strengthening the young Christian for spiritual combat" which would come with adolescence.

This new rite of confirmation, coupled with the practice of infant baptism and the new eucharistic piety which surrounded the Mass, separated first Communion from baptism. Though baptized infants were often brought to Communion well into the sixteenth century, thirteenth-century decrees forbid Communion prior to confirmation, linking "confirmation" with the "age of discretion." The rationale behind this development was based upon a new scrupulosity about the mystery of the Mass: Baptized children were not to commune until they were old enough to "discern the bread as the Body of Christ." Infant baptism, when practiced with confirmation, not only had the effect of disjoining baptism from the gift of the Holy Spirit and of ending the catechumenate but also had the effect of separating baptism from admission to the Lord's Table. Baptism was no longer an obvious part of Christian initiation. In fact, except as a bath to wash away original sin, it was not apparent what baptism actually accomplished or signified for the Christian in relationship to the Christian community. Like the Mass, baptism had become an individualized experience. For most baptisms, no one was present except parents and godparents; this practice removed the beginning of the Christian's individual pilgrimage from the community. Baptism had become little more than a rite which celebrated birth into society as a whole rather than initiation into a transforming community of faith.

In other words, the fragmentation of Christian initiation in the Middle Ages paralleled the fragmentation of the Christian community in the Mass. Having lost the older conflicts between the church and the world, the church now focused its worship life upon conflicts within the self. The growing introspection and individualism of the day were reinforced by celebration of objectified worship acts which were mainly valued for their subjective effect. An almost exclusive focus upon the Passion of Christ as the main significance of Christ's work was complemented by the almost exclusive preoccupation with individual sinfulness as the chief object of Christ's work. A fixation with the problem of individual sinfulness, a focusing upon the Mass and baptism as means of grace for the forgiveness of individual sinfulness, and the notion that the Christian. life was mostly concerned with eradicating individual sinfulness led to a liturgical life which, while it was lively, even beautiful in some of its more sublime expressions, was severely limited in its appropriation of the faith and tragically deficient in its expressions of liturgy as the work of all God's people.

Reform was needed, and reformation was soon to come.

Pulpit from Isle of Wight

Reformation and Reaction: The Sixteenth Century

6

On the Eve of All Saints Day in 1517, an Augustinian monk named Martin Luther nailed his Ninety-five Theses to the door of Castle Church in Wittenburg. In nailing his theses to the door, Luther was fulfilling his office of *doctor ecclesiae*. As a doctor of the church, he had taken vows to defend the church against false doctrine. In the Theses Luther launched a stinging barrage, principally aimed at the sale of indulgences which arose out of the medieval theology of penance. Church reform, church dissolution, and church reaction thus began. The storm had broken.

But it was almost six years later before Luther made his first attempt at worship reform. His primary concern was doctrine—asserting the primacy of the Scriptures and the doctrines of justification by faith and the priesthood of believers against the scholastic medieval understanding of the church and its ministry. Luther, like nearly all of his fellow reformers, primarily sought reform of church doctrine and polity and was only secondarily interested in worship as it related to these central concerns. The Reformers' creativity and sensitivity in matters of faith and doctrine far outweighed their abilities as reformers of worship.

This lack of creativity in the area of worship may be attributed to a number of reasons. First, all the Reformers believed in Luther's *sola scriptura* principle, that is, the Scriptures are the supreme authority in questions of faith and doctrine—neither the present officials nor the past traditions of the church outweigh scriptural authority. Yet, as we have seen in earlier chapters, the New Testament does not provide well-delineated liturgical forms. Liturgical revision which attempts to base itself solely upon Scripture is a risky undertaking. Second, because the Reformers lacked materials on the actual worship practices of the early church, any attempt on their part to establish worship in conformity with the most primitive practices of the church was doomed to failure. The Latin liturgy of the Middle Ages was the sole form of worship known to them. This led them to make serious historical errors in their attempts to restore purer earlier usages. Third, in a curious way, in some of their worship reforms, even some of their more radical revisions, the Reformers often accentuated some of the most limited aspects of medieval worship rather than fundamentally correcting medieval abuses. In their lack of interest in the corporate worship of the Christian community, their emphasis upon the role of the clergy in worship, their stress upon the sins of individuals, and their preoccupation with the Passion of Christ as the central fact of the Christ story, the Reformers were closer to their medieval predecessors in the church than to their more primitive forebears whom they admired but were unable to emulate.

Lutheran Reforms

The true strengths, as well as some of the most glaring weaknesses of Reformation liturgical reform can be seen by looking at the rather conservative reforms of baptism and the

Lord's Supper which were attempted by Martin Luther. Luther never questioned that the sacraments were a means of God's grace. Rather, Luther objected to the idea of the Mass as a propitiatory sacrifice because, in his eyes, it promoted a false religiosity and pietistic abuses. His main assault was not even so much upon the official eucharistic theology of his day as upon the popular misconception of the Mass as a daily sacrificing of Christ at the altar. Rather than view the Mass as a *sacrificium* (humanity's gift to God), Luther stressed the Mass as a *testamentum* (God's gift to humanity). For Luther, it would be idolatrous to regard the Mass as an *opus bonum*, as our good work, since this would be setting our human acts in place of God's act of grace in Christ. We are saved by grace, not by our good works, not even by our good works in worship. While Christians do offer themselves and their "sacrifice of praise and thanksgiving" to God in service before the altar, they in no way repeat or add to the once-and-for-all sacrifice of Christ or gain any merit by offering their gifts at the altar.

Luther, like other Reformers, continuing the development of late medieval theology, tied Christ's sacrifice principally to his atoning and redeeming death upon the cross rather than to the whole life and work of Christ. The old Passion-crucifixion emphasis of medieval theology thus continues in Luther. For Luther, the work of Christ on the cross is a finished act of reconciliation which calls forth only, but most assuredly, a continuous response from those who have been reconciled. Thus, the Eucharist is a human *response* to a divine gift. We receive more in Communion than we give.

Because of this theological position, when Luther turned his hand to reforming the Mass, he was forced to eliminate any suggestion of sacrifice from the Mass. In the beginning Luther was reluctant to tamper with the liturgy out of a concern, as he said, "for the weaker brethren." He first advocated and helped develop a weekday service of Scripture reading and preaching which was to educate people in true doctrine and to prepare them for more meaningful participation in the Sunday Mass. But in 1523, when one of his disciples, Andreas Carlstadt, began to make radical changes in the Mass, Luther was compelled to publish his own ideas on worship reform lest reform be undertaken by (in his words) "ignorant and mindless innovators." This *Formula Missae* was a conservative revision of the Mass. The Latin and most of the vestments and ceremonials of the older service were retained. His main revision was in the way of deletion. In order to counter what he believed to be the erroneous doctrines of eucharistic sacrifice, merit, and transubstantiation, Luther eliminated the offertory, directing that the bread and wine be prepared during the singing of the Creed so as to eliminate any hint that the offertory was prelude to a propitiatory sacrifice. He also eliminated the fraction (the breaking of the bread), objecting to the allegorism which had been attached to this symbolic act. This was a drastic deletion since, from the earliest times, the fraction was a major part of the Eucharist and an act of obvious biblical significance.

Rather curiously, he did retain the elevation of the bread during the singing of the Sanctus in spite of fierce objections to the practice on the part of some of his fellow Reformers. Luther retained the elevation since it was the only part of the older Mass in which the average person participated. Luther also saw the elevation as a symbolic witness to the presence of Christ in the eucharistic elements. While he denied transubstantiation, Luther stressed Christ's "ubiquity," that is, Christ is present everywhere at all times, but Christ is truly, really, and especially present in his full nature in the bread and wine of the Eucharist. This theory of ubiquity is Luther's attempt to affirm the real presence in the Eucharist without advocating transubstantiation. While Christ's presence in the Eucharist is real, Luther avoided scholastic attempts to define precisely the nature of the presence, being content, as was Calvin, to let the final nature of the presence be known only to God.

But the most radical change in the otherwise conservative *Formula Missae* was Luther's reduction of the canon to the words of institution, the recitation of the words and actions of Jesus in the Last Supper. This focus on the words of institution is in accord with Luther's *sola scriptura* principle and Luther's stress on the *testamentum,* since they speak explicitly of the "cup of the New Testament," the promises of God rather than the works of persons.

But in this radical revision of the central prayer of the Mass, Luther is as much within late medieval tradition as against it. The old debates over the "moment of consecration" had finally settled upon the words of institution as the high point of the Mass. (Aquinas had even said that a mass is valid if nothing else but the words are repeated!) Also, in Luther's stripping away of everything but the words, the medieval emphasis upon the substitutionary atonement of Christ and the forgiveness of sins as the central work of Christ was not only continued but also even accentuated. The isolation of the *Verba Christi* and limitation of the eucharistic prayer to the recitation of these *Verba* became the distinguishing characteristic of all later Lutheran liturgies. It was a radical change, but it was one which merely brought to a conclusion developments which had been going on throughout the Middle Ages.

As things turned out, Luther's first attempt at liturgical revision in the *Formula Missae* failed to meet the worship needs of the reform movement which was now sweeping across Germany. The Mass was still in Latin and was too conservative for many. In 1526, Luther issued his *Deutsche Messe*, a vernacular mass which was to be a kind of folk mass to educate the unlearned. In the *Deutsche Messe*, Luther continued his principle of reform by deletion, deleting various parts like the Gloria in Excelsis and the eucharistic Nicene Creed (which he replaced with the baptismal Apostles' Creed). Luther's main creative contribution to worship reform and the involvement of the laity was his use of popular German hymns in this service, thus restoring congregational music to the Eucharist, a contribution which was to become a singularly important facet of Protestant worship.

By reducing the canon to Jesus' words of institution, Luther greatly truncated the eucharistic prayer and eliminated all the other traditional themes associated with this prayer. Moreover, his liturgy tended to be pedagogical and didactic, forsaking older poetic images in the interest of tireless instruction and edification of the congregation in matters of correct doctrine. Because he had deleted many traditional parts of the service, the sermon not only was moved to greater prominence in Sunday worship, but it also dominated worship. The sermon became the center of most Protestant worship, the climax of the service for which the Lord's Supper appeared, in practice, as an appendage.

Luther did stress the importance of Communion, ruling that some and preferably all of the congregation should receive both the bread and the wine at each celebration. But we must remember that for almost a thousand years the laity of the Western church had communed infrequently. Noncommunicating, in the medieval tradition, became a problem for Luther's followers since tradition was difficult to overcome. Luther was forced to adapt his wishes to the people's limitations. He directed that those who wished to communicate should inform the pastor before the service. If no one so indicated, the pastor was to proceed with a Service of the Word— basically an ante-Communion with prayer, Scripture, hymns, and sermon. Unfortunately, this truncated service became the norm in most Lutheran churches. This was true in many Protestant churches for some of the same reasons which blocked Luther's attempts to restore more frequent Lord's Supper celebrations.

The same year that he published his *Formula Missae* Luther issued a much abbreviated baptismal rite. While he purged baptism of the medieval blessing of the water, he added a beautiful "Flood Prayer" which not only drew upon the Flood and the Exodus as antetypes of baptism but also restored an emphasis upon baptism as death and resurrection:

> Almighty everlasting God, you of your justice did destroy by the flood the unfaithful world, and of your mercy did save faithful Noah, even his family of eight persons, and did drown in the Red Sea hard-hearted Pharaoh with all his army, and did lead your people Israel safely through it; thereby you did figure the washing of your holy baptism. And by the baptism of your dear Son, our Lord Jesus Christ, you did sanctify the Jordan and all waters for a saving flood and an ample washing away of sins. We beseech you, for your infinite mercy, that you will mercifully look upon this *N.*, and bless him with true faith in the spirit, that by this wholesome laver all that was born in him from Adam and which he himself has added unto it may be drowned and submerged, and that he may be separated from the unfaithful and preserved in the holy ark of Christendom dry and safe, and being fervent in spirit and joyful through hope may ever serve thy name so that he may attain everlasting life with all the faithful, through Jesus Christ our Lord. Amen.[1]

In 1526, Luther complemented his *Deutsche Messe* with a simplified baptismal rite which omitted nearly all baptismal ceremonial, such as the use of oil and the gift of the candle. The naming of the child was linked with the application of water. Like all other Reformers, Lutherans rejected belief in the damnation of unbaptized infants as well as the related practice of baptism by lay persons. They allowed for private baptisms only in extreme

[1] Marion J. Hatchett, *Sanctifying Life, Time and Space* (New York: A Crossroad Book, imprint of The Seabury Press, Inc., 1976), p. 100. From *Sanctifying Life, Time, and Space* by Marion J. Hatchett, copyright © 1976 by The Seabury Press, Inc. Reprinted by permission of the publisher.

circumstances. While these changes were helpful in removing baptism from its preoccupation with questions of an individual's original sin and damnation and setting it back in the context of the congregation, fundamental problems remained with the practice of infant baptism. Infant baptism was never questioned by the major Reformers simply because the Reformers assumed that, historically, the church had always followed the practice. Theologically, the baptism of infants was also a vivid symbolic illustration of the Reformers' belief in "justification by faith."

One reason infant baptism continued to be problematic was because the Reformers did not restore infant Communion. While Luther rejected confirmation as being "mumbo-jumbo" which was "unknown to God" and which added nothing that was not already given in baptism, he continued the practice of delaying the Communion of baptized infants. Typical of the didacticism and pedagogical concern of the Reformers, Luther devised "catechisms" which attempted to explain the fundamentals of the faith and the sacraments, specifying that children should learn this "catechism" before being admitted to Communion. The practice of delayed Communion continued the unfortunate separation of baptism from admission to the Lord's Table, thus continuing to obscure baptism's significance as the rite of Christian initiation. The Reformers failed to see that, to be consistent, the continuance of infant baptism virtually necessitated the restoration of infant Communion.

As important as Luther's reforms were, the worship of the majority of Protestant Christianity was destined to be influenced by a more radical, more fundamental Reformer—Zwingli of Zurich.

Zwingli

Not long after Luther posted his Ninety-five Theses, Huldreich Zwingli, a priest in Zurich, launched the more radical Swiss Reformation. While he died relatively early in the Reformation (1531), Zwingli succeeded in founding the Reformed church, thus beginning a lively family of liturgies which spread throughout the world under the influence of a Frenchman, John Calvin.

Unlike Luther, Zwingli's theological views, particularly his views on worship, were thoroughly radical and in great opposition to traditional Christianity. While most later Protestants rejected Zwingli's theology, his ideas on worship, particularly his minimalist view of the sacraments, affected, to some degree, all non-Roman Western churches.

God, for Zwingli, is pure, transcendent spirit. Therefore, material elements like bread and wine could never be instruments of God's grace. While Scripture, the supreme and sole authority for Zwingli, does stress both (and, for Zwingli, *only*) baptism and the "Lord's Supper" (the Pauline designation for the Eucharist which was popular among the Reformers), these acts are only "pledges," or "signs," of what God has long ago done through Christ for us. The Lord's Supper is only a kind of visual aid, a "memorial," a helpful reminder of God's grace and forgiveness—not the conveyor of grace and forgiveness. Participation in the rites of baptism or the Lord's Supper is merely a demonstration, a public testimony of a person's faith in Christ.

While Luther believed the Lord's Supper was our "sacrifice of praise and thanksgiving," so opposed was Zwingli to the idea of eucharistic sacrifice that he purged any mention of sacrifice, Christ's or ours, from his Lord's Supper. While he did affirm, to some degree, the presence of Christ at the Eucharist, he denied Luther's idea of "ubiquity." Zwingli wanted nothing to detract from the transcendence of Christ, even though he did say that Christ's spiritual nature could be present among the believers at the meal but not in any way *in* the meal.

Somewhat inevitably, Zwingli's extreme views on the Lord's Supper led to his rejection of the Eucharist as the normal Sunday activity of Christians. He decreed that the Lord's Supper be celebrated only four times a year and only as an addition to his primary "preaching service." Quarterly Communion became the standard practice, not only in Reformed churches but eventually in many Lutheran, Free, and Anglican churches as well. While Zwingli may have believed that infrequent Communion restored the Lord's Supper to greater significance, the evidence in most Protestant churches which adopted the practice is decidedly to the contrary.

In his preaching service, Zwingli eliminated all music, vestments, the altar, and most congregational responses. His services were even more pedagogical than Luther's. The congregation's duty was to listen, to be edified, and to be corrected by the preacher. In his stress upon the Word and a rational response to the Word, in his view of the sacraments as mere visual aids to recollection and understanding, Zwingli was more a child of the emerging Enlightenment than a restorer of ancient practices. For Zwingli, the main response of the congregation was the response of faith—faith which was defined in increasingly rational, subjective, passive terms. All worship activity before or in place of this inner "faith" was merely self-delusion; it was diversion from the true purpose of worship rather than worship.

Zwingli's Lord's Supper, in its final German form of 1525, followed Luther's approach of drastic reduction of the canon down to the words of institution. The prayers for the service were strongly didactic, instructing the congregation in the meaning of the service. The epistle lesson was always Paul on the Last Supper from First Corinthians, and the Gospel was always John 6. Communion began with a strong exhortation which explained the Reformed interpretation of Communion followed by the Reformed practice of "fencing the table," in which all were warned not to come forward to Communion "unworthily." Communion was received seated, an attempt by Zwingli to give the Eucharist the feeling of a fellowship meal rather than a sacred rite. He specified that simple wooden vessels should be used, elements should be placed upon a simple table with the people seated round about, ministers should wear everyday black academic gowns, and the service should be led in "a loud clear voice, so that all the people may know what is done."

Anyone familiar with Protestantism's elevation of preaching as the major worship event, the almost complete lack of lay involvement in worship, and the emphasis upon education and moral exhortation of the laity through the liturgy can readily see the lasting influence of Zwingli.

Calvin

The third major personality of the continental Reformation was John Calvin of Geneva. While Calvin made the most significant contributions to Protestant theology and church government of the sixteenth-century Reformers, he showed little interest in liturgy.

Unlike Zwingli's rather humanistic view, Calvin's high doctrine of the sacraments strongly affirmed the sacraments as "means of grace." But, unlike Luther, he avoided a doctrine of the eucharistic real presence which was based upon a theory of objective realism. "I would rather experience it than understand it," Calvin said. For Calvin, Christ was really and fully present in the Lord's Supper by virtue of the power of the Holy Spirit. The believer, therefore, participates really but "spiritually" in the presence of Christ when the Lord's Supper is celebrated. The presence is real, but it is a spiritual presence. Calvin's doctrine of the eucharistic presence is somewhere between Luther's and Zwingli's.

Like Luther, Calvin wanted the Lord's Supper to be the primary, normal Sunday morning form of worship. But when he attempted to restore the weekly celebration of the Lord's Supper at the Protestant Reformed Church in Geneva, ardent disciples of Zwingli defeated his efforts. When he went to Strasbourg, he met similar resistance due to the Zwinglian leanings of Strasbourg's chief minister in the 1530s, Martin Bucer. Bucer had devised a service which sought to mediate between Lutheranism and Zwinglianism. Strasbourg followed the Lutheran pattern of a Sunday service within the context of the Eucharist, but full Communion was celebrated only monthly.

Eventually, whether out of realism about the people's limitations or lack of strong interest in liturgical reform, Calvin contented himself with a compromise solution when he returned to Geneva in 1541. While he had hoped to institute weekly Communion, full Communion was celebrated only once a month at Geneva. On other Sundays, a rather long preaching service was used which included the Reformed practice of singing from the Psalter in meter. Calvinist worship tended toward austere intellectualism, didacticism, verbosity, and little congregational participation. Communion was usually received standing or seated at tables rather than seated at the pews as the Zwinglians had done. Reformed churches were uniform in their dislike of kneeling for Communion, rejecting the practice because of its sacerdotal connotations.

Calvin's baptismal theology was as strong as Luther's. His baptismal services were similar to Luther's, characterized mainly by deletions rather than additions with a new emphasis upon baptism as reception into God's covenant of grace, a natural counterpart of Calvinistic covenant theology.

European Free Churches

While Lutherans and Reformed churches had deep misgivings about the form and content of the medieval liturgies, they never doubted the value of liturgy itself. While the Reformers reintroduced variety and adaptability into Christian worship, their services followed set patterns. There were variations and alternatives for their prayers, but the content of prayers was carefully fixed. Liturgies were officially (governmentally) approved and established for all the churches within a given state in the interest of civil order and ecclesiastical uniformity.

But in the ferment of Reformation, small sects arose which demanded even more freedom in matters of doctrine and worship. These "Free churches," as they were eventually designated, were made up of the Anabaptists on the Continent and the Independents, Separatists, and (eventually) the Puritans in England and Scotland.

Free churches generally maintained that the form of worship was a matter of congregational choice; that a fixed, printed order of worship was a hindrance to true Christian worship; and that fixed prayers should be replaced with extemporary, "free" prayers which came "from the heart" and were open to the "leading of the Spirit." Lengthy Scripture readings and even more lengthy sermons were the main content of their services. All "outward forms," such as vestments, ceremonial, and the church year, were uniformly rejected.

Baptism and the Lord's Supper were practiced in all Free churches. But they were done in the simplest manner possible, accompanied by recital of Scripture and extemporary prayer. The congregation remained seated for Communion. Free churches tended to reject the idea that baptism and the Lord's Supper were "sacraments"—divine acts which especially conveyed divine grace. For most of them, baptism and the Lord's Supper were "ordinances"—human activities ordained by Christ for our edification and fellowship, acts which follow faith rather than precede faith, signs of the presence of faith in the life of the individual believer rather than conveyors of faith. While many Free churches retained infant baptism, the Anabaptists regarded the baptism of infants as contrary to New Testament practice and a sign of the ultimate compromise of the church and its gospel. For them, baptism must be preceded by a personal confession of faith.

They baptized only adults, usually by immersion after a confession of faith, and rebaptized (hence the name "Anabaptists") those who had been baptized as infants. Anabaptist leader Menno Simons, in denying baptism as a sacrament or as a means of regeneration, wrote:

> We are not regenerated because we have been baptized, . . . but we are baptized because we have been regenerated by faith and the Word of God (I Pet. 1:23). Regeneration is not the result of baptism, but baptism the result of regeneration. This can indeed not be controverted by any man, or disproved by the Scriptures.[2]

Throughout the sixteenth and seventeenth centuries, the Free churches suffered persecution not only at the hands of Roman Catholics but also by established Protestant churches, such as the Lutherans, Calvinists, and Anglicans. During these persecutions, many Free Church people fled to America. Their presence in this new land accounted for the determinedly anti-establishment, voluntaristic, Free Church leanings of American Protestantism. To this day, even among those with "liturgical" roots, such as Methodists and Presbyterians, many American Protestants are suspicious of liturgical service books, sacraments, fixed prayers, and liturgical ornamentation and regard the manner of Sunday worship to be the prerogative of each local congregation and its pastor. This is, in great part, a legacy of the Free churches.

Reaction

While the Reformers' work rapidly dissolved the Western church, Rome vigorously reacted in hopes of restoring and sustaining the old order. From 1545 to 1563, the Council of Trent labored to stem the tide.

Unfortunately, in matters of worship, the so-called Counter-Reformation did little to reform. While some at the Council noted the need to deal with the problems of votive masses, the cluttered church year, and infrequent lay Communion, no significant decrees were issued in regard to liturgical reform. The Council of Trent mostly solidified medieval liturgical doctrines, defending them as absolute truth from which no deviation could be permitted. Whatever the Reformers questioned—transubstantiation, the Mass as a propitiatory sacrifice, the role of the

[2] H. S. Bender, *Menno Simons' Life and Writings*, with Simons' writings trans. John Horsch (Scottdale, Pa.: Mennonite Publishing House, 1936), p. 78.

hierarchical priesthood, the sacramental system—the Council defended as divinely ordained.

Liturgical matters were left mostly to the pope. In 1570, Pius V promulgated a uniform missal for the entire Roman church. This missal generally ended any local adaptation or variation in the church's liturgy except for a few cathedrals which were allowed to continue some ancient local customs. The uniform missal had the effect not only of unifying the Roman liturgy but also of solidifying it, rigidifying it into an officially decreed matter in which even the slightest deviation was forbidden. The medieval rite, with its limitations, problems, and particular style of worship, became fixed as the absolute norm for Roman Catholic worship everywhere and for all time. In 1588, Sixtus V created the Congregation of Rites to insure that the church's worship was the same in every church in Roman Christendom. Even the mere translation of the canon into the vernacular, not only for the purpose of worship but even for instruction and understanding, was expressly forbidden. No real revision was to take place in Roman Catholic worship for nearly four hundred years.

The Counter-Reformation's attempt to stem the tide of reform by imposing rigid uniformity perpetuated some of the worst problems of the medieval period. The Mass was even more the priest's act, a "divine drama," a beautiful mystery on the stage of a Baroque theater which was designed to confound and convert an age of increasing rationalism and skepticism. Elaborate musical settings for the Mass—often to instrumental accompaniment, pomp, ornamentation, and Baroque architectural decoration— were combined in a theatrical spectacle before the faithful. Extraliturgical devotions, such as the Adoration of the Blessed Sacrament and the cult of the Rosary, increased in importance as substitutes for the true participation of the laity in the Mass.

Summary

While the Reformers succeeded in achieving more congregational participation in worship, the basic worship attitudes continued to be individualistic and subjective. The role of the congregation was still a passive one. While unity of word and table was stressed by Luther and Calvin, they were unable to achieve it in practice. The sermon was restored to prominence in the liturgy, a prominence which tended toward dominance in most Protestant worship. Luther reformed the liturgical calendar, restoring the earlier Christological focus. Other Reformers generally rejected the use of the church year altogether, feeling that it was too corrupt to be reformed and that it obscured the centrality of Sunday. Luther and Calvin gave baptism more balance in relation to original sin than was the case in the Middle Ages. But challenges by Anabaptists and their heirs raised fundamental questions about baptism and eventually bitterly divided Protestants on the issue of infant versus adult baptism. Western Christendom was rent asunder, split between a wide variety of Protestant options which ranged from Lutheran conservatism to Anabaptist radicalism on the one hand and a rigidly reactionary Roman Catholic church on the other.

Old Baptist Meetinghouse, 1796,
Yarmouth, Maine

Prayer Books and Puritans:
The English Reformation

7

While Europe was in the throes of reformation and reaction, the church in England was becoming the Church of England. Henry VIII's break with the papacy was more political than theological. The governance of the English church changed from the pope to English hands, but the doctrine and liturgy of this national "Catholic" church changed little from that of the Roman medieval church until Henry's death in 1547.

During his life, Henry's conservatism in matters of doctrine and liturgy kept changes to a minimum. At his death, when Edward VI came to the throne, Englishmen who had caught the

Reformation fever saw their chance to establish a Reformed church in England. Led by the archbishop of Canterbury, Thomas Cranmer, and the future bishop of London, Nicholas Ridley, they sought a moderate, middle-of-the-road brand of reform. Like Calvin, whose disciples had influenced them, they opposed the medieval doctrines of the Mass as sacrifice and the doctrine of transubstantiation but were not opposed to the Eucharist as a "sacrifice of praise and thanksgiving" and the idea of the real presence of Christ in the Eucharist. They opposed medieval clericalism but, unlike the Calvinists, believed in the validity of the priesthood and in church governance by bishops. They disliked elaborate medieval ceremonial but did not wish to eliminate all ceremony. These reformers stood between the English conservatives, who liked Henry's position of as little divergence as possible from medieval practices, and the extreme Protestants, who were Calvinist in matters of doctrine and Zwinglian in matters of liturgy. The conservatives had little influence in the government but great support from the English masses. The extreme Protestants were a dedicated minority who over a period of time gained control of the government and greatly changed English worship.

Beginning in 1547, Scripture was read in English at High Mass. That same year, Parliament decreed (in hopes of countering the radical sacramental views of the extreme Protestants) that both the wine and the bread should be received by communicants at the Mass. But, as we learned in chapter 5, the cup had been withheld from the laity in the Western church since the 1200s. The medieval Latin Mass had no provision for Communion of both elements by the laity. This dilemma gave Archbishop Cranmer the opportunity to undertake, not a minor revision of the old Mass, but a major reformation of English worship. In 1548, Cranmer presented an Order of Communion in English which included exhortations regarding the proper preparation for receiving "Holy Communion" (as the English Reformers were now referring to the Mass), an invitation, general confession, absolution, and "Comfortable Words" (scriptural passages stressing forgiveness), followed by Cranmer's much beloved "Prayer of Humble Access":

> WE do not presume to come to this thy table (o mercifull lorde) trusting in our owne righteousness, but in thy manifold & great mercies: we be not woorthie so much as to gather up the cromes under

thy table, but thou art the same lorde whose propertie is alwayes to haue mercie: Graunt us therefore (gracious lorde) so to eate the fleshe of thy dere sonne Jesus Christ, and to drynke his bloud in these holy Misteries, that we may continuallye dwell in hym, and he in us, that oure synfull bodyes may bee made cleane by his body, and our soules washed through hys most precious bloud. Amen.[1]

Then followed the people's Communion in both bread and wine and a blessing. The remainder of the service followed the ending of the Latin Mass.

This service prepared the way for the composition of a full book of services and prayers, a book which condensed the numerous and unwieldy worship books which priests had been using to lead worship and would, for the first time, put the texts of services in the hands of each worshiper. Gutenberg's invention had thus made possible the most important single event in the reformation of the worship of English-speaking people—the publication of the *Book of Common Prayer*.

The 1549 Prayer Book

On Whitsunday, 1549, the use of the first *Book of Common Prayer* was required in English churches by the compulsory Act of Uniformity. Cranmer drew upon an amazing variety of sources— the early fathers, Lutheran church orders, a Spanish cardinal's Breviary, Eastern Orthodox liturgies, old Gallic rites—integrating this material into the Sarum Rite, the Roman rite as it had been adapted to English usage at Salisbury, the chief source of this first English prayer book. Cranmer stated the principles which guided him in the selection of material for the book: (1) "grounded in holy Scripture," (2) "agreeable to the order of the primitive church," (3) "unifying to the Kingdom," and (4) "edifying" to the people. In the book which grew out of these principles we see both Cranmer's genius as a liturgical reformer and his weaknesses.

Like his fellow Reformers on the Continent, Cranmer wanted his services to be "grounded in holy Scripture" and "agreeable to the order of the primitive church." In his service "The Supper of the Lorde, and the holy Communion, commonly called the Masse," his main emphases were upon the benefits of Communion and the necessity of the people receiving the sacrament. No

[1] Bard Thompson, *Liturgies of the Western Church* (New York: The World Publishing Co., 1961), p. 261.

Eucharist should be offered at which only the priest communed. This was intended to restore the New Testament emphasis on the benefits of Communion and its ethical, pastoral consequences and to move away from the medieval preoccupation with eucharistic presence and sacrifice. The 1549 book also specified that larger and thicker eucharistic wafers were to be used. (Later books specified that any good wheat bread was adequate for Communion.) The bread should be placed in the people's mouths, not as a concession to the medieval custom, but to ensure that the people would not carry the bread from the church and put it to superstitious use. (Subsequent prayer books decreed that the bread be placed in the people's hands.) We also know, from the size of the Communion flagons (pitchers) in this period that a comparatively large quantity of wine was consumed at Communion. The language of all services was simplified and made more direct. While Cranmer never lapsed into the rigid biblicism of some of the continental Reformers (because of his respect for church tradition), he did eliminate elaborate ceremonial in order to make his book more acceptable to reformed churchmen in England.

In the baptismal service, he purged the breathing on the child, the giving of salt, some of the anointings, and the gift of the candle. But he retained the sign of the cross on the candidate's forehead and the vesting of the newly baptized in a white gown. Confirmation was retained without the questionable medieval practice of anointing but with the laying on of hands.

Throughout his 1549 prayer book, Cranmer sought the *via media*—the "middle way." England was deeply divided over matters of religion between the conservative Catholics, the reform-minded moderates, and the extreme Protestants. Knowing that Henry VIII had attempted doctrinal unity and had failed, Cranmer sought religious unity through common worship rather than doctrinal consensus. His *Book of Common Prayer* had to be acceptable to as many people as possible. This accounts for the book's occasional ambivalent maneuvering between conflicting doctrinal and liturgical positions. For instance, Cranmer downplayed the offertory because it was too closely associated with the medieval concept of the eucharistic sacrifice. When the offering is mentioned, Cranmer stresses the people's giving of alms. He forbade the elevation of the host. In his "Prayer of Consecration" (as he calls the eucharistic prayer), he carefully (almost laboriously) emphasizes that our remembrance is of Christ's past sacrifice, not ours. But he does allow the people's "sacrifice of praise and thanksgiving" as well as our offering of "our selves, our souls and bodies, to be a reasonable, holy, and living sacrifice unto thee. . . ." The most creative and, as it turned out, most significant of Cranmer's liturgical contributions were the Morning and Evening Prayer.

In the monastic communities, in the Divine Office (chapter 5) corporate prayer was offered on eight different occasions throughout each day. The practice probably originated in the private devotions of the Jews in which daily personal prayers were offered at various times. During the fourth century, as monasticism flowered, the monks created daily corporate worship services consisting mostly of Psalms and prayers: Nocturns were said before dawn, lauds at dawn, prime, terce, sext, and none at the first, third, sixth, and ninth hours of the day, vespers at twilight, and compline at bedtime. Each week the entire Psalter would be recited during these services. By the late Middle Ages even the secular clergy read these daily services alone or in groups, using the Breviary. Some lay people also attended lauds or vespers on Sundays or holy days. The services were to be additional opportunities for laity to worship before or after the Eucharist rather than substitutes for the Eucharist.

In the 1549 prayer book, Cranmer drew heavily upon these daily monastic prayer services when he formulated Morning and Evening Prayer (matins and evensong). Cranmer hoped to reinforce the Reformation belief in the priesthood of the laity by liberating the Divine Office from clerical and monastic dominance and giving it back to the laity. He expected the laity to come together daily for Psalms, lessons, and prayers. Since monasticism had been outlawed in England in the 1530s, a void had been created in the daily worship of those laity who formerly attended monastic services. Through Morning and Evening Prayer, the laity could now worship daily in their own parish churches. Lay people could even lead these services when a priest was absent. On Sundays, matins could simply precede the Eucharist.

Cranmer's intentions for daily English corporate worship were never fully realized. The laity had not the inclination nor the time to worship twice daily in their parish churches. Morning and Evening Prayer became services mainly for the clergy to read each day within their churches with infrequent participation by the laity. On Sundays, however, Morning and Evening Prayer were almost too successful. Since the majority of medieval English Christians only participated in Communion once a year, there was no tradition of regular lay Communion. Cranmer's insistence that every person in the congregation should receive holy Communion each Sunday was never followed.

Anglican Sunday worship developed a noneucharistic pattern: Morning Prayer, the litany (responsive prayer), the ante-Communion (the first part of the service up to the offertory), and, lastly, a sermon and prayer. Sunday worship became a Service of the Word: a rather dry, didactic, verbose service of Scripture, prayer, and sermon. The full Communion service was celebrated only once a month at best, thrice yearly in most cases. Cranmer had done so well on Morning Prayer that it soon became the best loved of all the services in his *Book of Common Prayer*—a well-stated, biblically centered, restrained, balanced mode of worship which proved well suited to the English temperament and to English worship needs. It is an odd circumstance of liturgical history that the service which Cranmer designed to give daily worship back to the people had the effect of keeping regular Sunday Communion from the people for another three hundred years.

While the 1549 *Book of Common Prayer* became both the model and the source for all succeeding revisions of the Anglican prayer book, and while it represents a remarkable achievement in creating liturgies which are uniquely English and realistically reformed, in its own day the book was a failure. It failed because in its moderation, in its attempt to please all factions, like many such attempts at compromise, it succeeded in pleasing few and in alienating many. It also failed because the idea of a uniform, prescribed liturgy was too radical for a church which had, even in the medieval period, allowed much variety and local adaptation. Remember that the Roman Catholic church was never under a prescribed, carefully uniform liturgy until the decrees of Pius V in 1570.

For the reform-minded, the book was unacceptable because it failed to excise all suggestion of sacrifice and eucharistic presence. It allowed the retention of vestments and some ceremonial. Protestant extremists either ignored the book or modified it as they wished. Conservatives resisted the book for opposite reasons. An armed rebellion arose among the nobility and peasants in the south of England in protest of the book's removal of some devotional and ceremonial practices which were dear to the heart of the average person. To have the elevation of the host removed (the one part of the Mass in which the average person felt any real sense of participation—even if it was mostly visual participation), the masses for the dead eliminated, and the familiar ceremonial replaced by rather barren and colorless rites, was a great shock to conservative sensibilities.

But the political winds were shifting decidedly in the Protestants' favor. Henry VIII, hard pressed for funds, began a program of official plunder of the church's wealth which had accrued during the Middle Ages. He received warm support from radical Protestants in this endeavor since they saw this as a way to disarm the conservatives and strengthen the Protestant position. In the upheaval which followed, the conservatives who opposed the Crown's actions were either jailed or sent into exile on the Continent. More radical reformers were now on the rise. John Hooper, Miles Coverdale, and John Knox became new ecclesiastical advisers to the Crown. A new prayer book was demanded, but the bishops were reluctant to begin a new book so soon after the failure of the previous one. By 1552, when the bishops finally consented to produce a new and more Protestant book, they found that Cranmer was already at work on a second *Book of Common Prayer*.

The 1552 Prayer Book

While the chief source for the 1549 prayer book was the medieval Sarum Rite of Salisbury Cathedral, the 1552 book drew upon more Protestant sources. Cranmer's work in the first book had been severely criticized by some of the continental Reformers whom he respected, to say nothing of the barbs of the radical English Reformers. In addition to this criticism, Cranmer's work on the new book was heavily influenced by the new Zwinglian liturgies which European Protestant refugees brought with them when they fled to England. The second *Book of Common Prayer*, therefore, represents a decided move to the left in its theology and form.

But once again Cranmer ran into liturgical problems in trying to solve theological-political problems through the new prayer book. The 1552 prayer book was poorly constructed, fragmented in its approach to worship, and confused in its application of conflicting theological principles. The book's main problems occurred in its radical revision of "The Order for the Lord's Supper, or Holy Communion." (The designation "Mass" had been eliminated.)

In 1549, the presiding minister at Communion was to wear the traditional chasuble and alb. While the extreme Protestants would have liked Cranmer to eliminate all vestments, in 1552 he eliminated the older dress but substituted the white surplice over a cassock. The radicals had criticized the 1549 Communion for not being penitential enough; so, in 1552, Cranmer added a recital of the Decalogue (Ten Commandments) at the beginning of the service to replace the service music which he had been forced, by Protestant opinion, to delete. The service now had a decidedly penitential somberness about it, to say nothing of a rather verbose, didactic quality.

Having deemphasized the offertory in 1549, in this new Communion Cranmer now pleased the extremists by eliminating any mention of the bread and wine and by relating the offertory solely to the giving of alms. No hint of oblation or sacrifice could now be found in the service. The stress was upon the work of Christ upon the cross, with our response being solely a response of faith. It was the Protestant doctrine of justification by faith embodied in a eucharistic liturgy. When the elements were given to the people, no longer did the minister say, "The Body of our Lord Jesus Christ. . . . The Blood of our Lord Jesus Christ. . . ." Now only "Take and eat this. . . . Drink this in remembrance . . ." were used. Ordinary bread replaced unleavened eucharistic wafers.

But Cranmer refused to bow to all the extremists' wishes. He refused to delete the Lord's Prayer, which some Reformers considered "vain and repetitious." He moved it, however, from its historic position after the eucharistic prayer to a point after the Communion. Here, along with his prayer of thanksgiving (which the extremists continued to criticize because it expressed a belief in the eucharistic presence) and the Gloria in Excelsis (the one piece of liturgical music he retained even if it had never been in this position before), the Lord's Prayer contributed to an exceedingly long and rather anticlimactic ending for the service.

On the issue of kneeling to receive the elements, Cranmer

steadfastly refused to placate the Protestants and remove kneeling from the service. But extremists like John Knox and Bishop Hooper, after winning King Edward to their point of view, nearly succeeded in forcing Cranmer to delete kneeling. As a compromise, Cranmer offered his famous "Black Rubric" on the meaning of kneeling and placed it at the end of the Communion service. The rubric carefully denied that kneeling at Communion implied a belief in transubstantiation but allowed, even supported, kneeling as an appropriate posture from which to receive Communion. Kneeling for Communion not only signified continuity with older traditions but became another factor which contributed to the heavily penitential character of Cranmer's holy Communion. There is much truth to the observation that Reformers like Cranmer abolished the medieval sacrament of penance only to transform the Eucharist into a new rite of penance for Protestants!

This penitential emphasis also affected the services of Morning and Evening Prayer in the new book. To these services Cranmer added a penitential beginning—Opening Sentence, General Confession prayed by all, and Absolution by the priest—once again in order to please those Reformers who saw worship primarily as an occasion for an admission of sin and a call to repentance.

In his 1552 rites for baptism and confirmation, Cranmer removed all ceremonial except the sign of the cross in baptism (which he moved from its historic position to after the baptism) and the laying on of the bishop's hands in confirmation. Baptismal regeneration was stated explicitly. Confirmation was given a new rationale, one which was more in keeping with the Reformation view of the importance of catechetical instruction, public renewal of vows, and first admission to Communion.

The 1552 book was made compulsory by a second Act of Uniformity, but it endured only a year. The Marian reaction (under the rule of Queen Mary) swept it away and sent Reformers like Cranmer either to their deaths or to the Continent where they waited and absorbed even more Protestant zeal. In 1559, with Good Queen Bess on the throne and the Protestants back in power, a more rigidly reformed and less creative or unified prayer book was forced upon England. But the old piety was long in dying among the common people, many of whom simply withdrew from English parish worship. Catholic conservatives (though now a persecuted and inconsequential minority) and Puritans (who were gaining strength since the Protestant exile) were still unsatisfied.

Puritans and High Churchmen

"That imperfect book culled and picked out of that popish dunghill the Masse" was how the Puritan Party in Anglicanism looked upon the prayer book. They lay in wait for a time to finish the English Reformation. John Knox, while in exile in Geneva, issued a thoroughly reformed English liturgy which showed a growing Free Church influence. His *Forme of Prayers* (1556) was introduced by Knox when he returned after the death of Mary Tudor. Knox returned not to England but to Scotland where the Scots were busy carrying forth the reformation without the restraints which Elizabeth had imposed upon England. Under Knox, the Kirk of Scotland was formed—Presbyterian in polity, Calvinist in doctrine, Puritan in worship. Influenced by Knox, the Puritan Party also gained strength in the Church of England. It sought to "purify" English worship of all "nonbiblical" accretions. But Elizabeth resisted Puritan efforts, feeling that her realm desperately needed the unity of a common worship book.

At first the Puritans opposed in the prayer book such "popish" holdovers as kneeling for Communion, observance of saints' days, Communion of the sick (because it reminded them of the old private Mass), and ceremonial acts such as the giving of rings in marriage and the sign of the cross in baptism (most Puritans had no problems with infant baptism, interpreting it from a Calvinist perspective of bringing infants into the covenant of God). These acts were opposed because they were deemed to be contrary to Scripture.

Later, under the influence of Independents, Puritans developed a more Free Church approach, seeking to abolish prayer book worship altogether. When Elizabeth died in 1603, James I came to the throne. Since James had been a Presbyterian in Scotland, the Puritans welcomed James as a fellow reformer. But James was of little help to them. Along with a new authorized version of the Bible (1611), James did issue a new prayer book in 1604. But the new book was merely a mild attempt to appease the Puritans. Its changes were insignificant. Basically, the 1604 book was a new edition of the 1552 book. James was determined to make good Anglicans of the English Puritans and even attempted to recover the Scottish Kirk for Anglicanism. But Knoxian attitudes were too firmly entrenched in Scotland.

Under James's son, Charles I, the archbishop of Canterbury, William Laud, led a group within Anglicanism called the "High Churchmen." These "Laudian and Caroline Divines" had a high doctrine of the church, the ministry, and the sacraments, claiming that these things were of divine origin and should be given utmost prominence in church life. Their opponents, the "Low Churchmen," believed that the sacraments were human creations and that matters of personal morality, individual piety, and good deeds were more important. The Laudians remained within the Reformed camp, theologically. Their main concern was with modification of worship practices and patterns rather than change of the prayer book. While not forsaking their Reformed emphasis upon the Word, they hoped to reverse earlier Zwinglian tendencies in Anglicanism. Laudians advocated more ceremony and reverence for holy Communion and, in many places, succeeded in instituting monthly celebrations of the sacrament. Under the Laudians the "altar" replaced the Low Church Communion table, and railings were erected to enclose the chancel. These were architectural means of expressing Laudian high eucharistic theology.

But the Laudians also helped precipitate an open rebellion against the king and Anglicanism. Even though James I had not made much headway in getting the Scots to accept the *Book of Common Prayer,* in the 1620s and 1630s a small group of radically conservative Scots produced a prayer book for the Church of Scotland. It was even more traditionally Catholic than Cranmer's, and Archbishop Laud warned King Charles not to try to impose so radical a revision upon the Scots. But Charles imposed the book on July 23, 1637. On that day, when the dean of Edinburgh attempted to conduct services at Knox's old church, Saint Giles, using the new book, a young Scottish woman, Jenny Geddes, hurled a stool at the dean's head when he began reading from the dreaded book. The congregation then turned into a riotous mob, and the dean made a hasty retreat!

The result of Charles's misguided efforts was a bitter religious war between Scotland and England which became the civil war of the 1640s. The Puritan Party was to win the day. First Laud was beheaded, then King Charles. From 1649 to 1658 Oliver Cromwell led England. A conglomeration of Presbyterians and Independents became the official religion of Cromwell's Commonwealth. Anglicanism and Roman Catholicism were proscribed.

Without Anglicanism and the *Book of Common Prayer,* the Cromwellian Parliament issued *A Directory for the Public Worship of God.* The *Westminster Directory,* as it came to be called, was a worship book composed entirely of Puritan rubrics and suggestions for corporate worship but without the completely extemporaneous approach advocated by the Separatists. It forbade the use of wedding rings, vestments, creeds, the Lord's Prayer in the Eucharist, and (with the exception of metrical singing of the Psalms) discouraged *any* congregational participation in public worship.

If the *Directory* had survived, the worship of English Puritans might have retained some balance between extemporaneous worship and Anglican formalism. But the *Directory* was as short-lived as the Commonwealth. After Cromwell's death in 1658, his Commonwealth disintegrated, and the monarchy was restored in 1660 in the person of Charles II. Once again Anglicanism and its *Book of Common Prayer* became the established church and liturgy of England. The Presbyterians hoped to influence the revision of the prayer book. But they were now out of favor in an England exhausted by religious extremism and political upheaval. In 1662, a new edition of the prayer book was issued which was simply the 1552 book with a few additional rubrics and a number of minor linguistic alterations. The Puritan Party was, for all intents and purposes, forced out of the Church of England by the new Act of Uniformity which forbade any local variations in prayer book worship.

Among those who dissented from established Anglican worship were a group of English Separatists who fled to Holland with a former Anglican priest, John Smyth. Smyth, having reasoned that the Church of England was a "corrupt church," sought the source of that corruption. He concluded that it lay in the rite of initiation—baptism—which was being indiscriminately administered to all children in English parishes. Since the Church of England was no church, then its baptism was no real baptism. So Smyth baptized himself, an act which he interpreted not as *re*baptism (since, according to his reasoning, he had not yet been baptized) but as true Christian baptism. He also administered baptism to others in his group and thereby formed what many believe to be the origins of present-day Baptists.

Smyth's congregation in Holland abandoned Puritan Calvinist doctrines of salvation and adopted the more generous thought of the Dutchman, Arminius. Unlike the Calvinists, Arminians believed that humanity has the freedom to accept or reject God's offer of salvation. There is a "general election" by God of all people (hence, the name "General Baptists," as Smyth's group was eventually designated). Baptism is the rite of initiation, coming after conversion, which is interpreted as a free and conscious commitment of faith to Christ. Their Arminian position led Baptists to view worship primarily as human responsiveness to God rather than as God's activity toward humanity. Baptism is a sign of prior adult response to God rather than a "means of grace" signifying God's prior act of salvation.

In 1638 a separatist congregation in London rejected the baptism of infants in favor of believer's baptism, following essentially the same reasoning as Smyth's congregation. But through contact with an Anabaptist group in Holland, they also recovered the death-life baptismal image of Paul (see chapter 2). They adopted the Anabaptist practice of total immersion which was eventually adopted by nearly all Baptist groups. These London Baptists became known as the Particular Baptists because of their adherence to Calvinist soteriology.

Many early Baptists observed the Lord's Supper at least monthly, with nonmembers being dismissed before the Communion. Their eucharistic theology was thoroughly Zwinglian. Communion elements were passed to the pews by the minister or deacons of the congregation. From England and the Low Countries, these diverse groups of Baptists fled to America where they enjoyed religious freedom and had a major impact upon American religious life.

One of the most radical groups to emerge from the ferment of this period was the Quakers, or Society of Friends. They eliminated *all* "outward forms," all sacraments and ordinances, even the very use of words themselves in worship in favor of a silent waiting upon God in order to be fully open to the Spirit's leadings. Quakers felt that the Puritans, in their reliance on sermons and long (even if extemporaneous) prayers, were still depending upon "human inventions." The Spirit and its inspiration were the central facts of public worship for the Quakers, even more central than Scripture. For these attitudes, Quaker leader George Fox suffered persecution from his Puritan contemporaries as well as from the Anglicans.

Summary

The 1662 prayer book has continued as the worship book of Anglicans until the reforms of our century. Like all of its predecessors, the 1662 book stressed the Eucharist above preaching and emphasized corporate, scripturally grounded prayer above everything. But in actual Sunday practice, Anglicans failed to restore holy Communion to a central place in parish worship and to involve the people in truly common worship. For the next two centuries, English worship was characterized by long, dull, moralistic preaching and rather dry, verbose, pedestrian, nonsacramental, colorless liturgy.

It was this dryness, this flattened respectability and wordiness of English worship which a contemporary English poet protested when he lamented:

> The windless northern surge, the sea-gull's scream,
> And Calvin's kirk crowning the barren brae.
> I think of Giotto the Tuscan shepherd's dream,
> Christ, man and creature in their inner day.
> How could our race betray
> The Image, and the Incarnate One unmake
> Who chose this form and fashion for our sake?
>
> The Word made flesh here is made word again,
> A word made word. . . .[2]

In spite of its shortcomings as a movement of liturgical reform, Puritanism was, in great part, an attempt to enliven the dullness of establishment worship, an effort to introduce the warmth of feeling, the vibrant fellowship, and the vivid preaching which official Anglicanism lacked. These Puritan concerns were now transported to the New World by Congregationalists and Baptists where they took root and became influential in shaping the worship of American Protestantism.

Unfortunately, all too many English people, dismayed by the century of reforms and counterreforms, failing to understand what

[2] Edwin Muir, "The Incarnate One," *Collected Poems* (New York: Oxford University Press, 1965), p. 228. Copyright © 1960 by Willa Muir. Reprinted by permission of Oxford University Press, Inc.

all the theological fuss was about, enthusiastically adopted neither Anglicanism nor Puritanism and simply withdrew from active engagement in Sunday worship as the eighteenth century ended. This was the result, not so much of weaknesses within the prayer book itself, but, rather, weaknesses in the way it was introduced. The torpidity of Anglican worship (until the nineteenth century) is testimony to the ineffectiveness of liturgical reform by political coercion.

Rehoboth Methodist Church,
Union, West Virginia

Rationalists, Pietists, and Revivalists: After the Reformation

8

In the centuries after the Reformation, the modern world fully emerged as a fact to be confronted, resisted, or embraced within the worship of the church. Was the Reformation part of the Middle Ages or part of modern history? On the one hand, we have noted how Luther's liturgical reforms in their emphasis upon sin and grace, the atonement as the major work of Christ, and the Passion as the major part of the saving work were continuous with major emphases of older theology. From this point of view, Protestant reformers like Luther appear to bring to fruition developments which had been in progress during the Middle Ages rather than changing those developments in a very radical manner.

On the other hand, the Reformation did signal a new apprehension of the faith. The old sacramental system of the church had been broken. Baptism and the Lord's Supper were valued, but most Protestants tended to look upon them as signs of divine promises rather than as exclusive channels of divine grace. The Holy Spirit, most Protestants contended, freely used other means for its purposes. One comes to the faith mainly through the reading and hearing of the *Word* of God. The presence of Christ is primarily experienced as a direct, personal, and individual relationship rather than as the result of corporate experiences of corporate means of grace. In its rather humanistic, individualistic view of worship, the Reformation was part of the emerging modern world and its values; indeed, it contributed to the shaping of that world.

The liturgical developments of the post-Reformation period were the logical culmination of ideas which were given birth during the Reformation. Eventually the Reformers' liturgical weaknesses were to become Protestantism's glaring deficiencies. The Counter-Reformation's response to the Protestants became hardened reaction. The rise of modern science and philosophy, the radically different conditions of life in the New World, and the collapse of the old political order meant dramatic changes in the cultural context of European Christianity, cultural changes which greatly influenced Christian worship.

European Developments

It is an odd fact of liturgical history that European Free churches, which made few inroads into the European religious scene, eventually became the predominant factor in the worship of most European Protestants. Even though the Free churches were vigorously persecuted by Lutheran, Reformed, and Anglican established churches, by the eighteenth and nineteenth centuries Free Church worship ideas dominated many Lutheran and Reformed churches (with the exception of the Scandinavian Lutherans).

The Sunday service which had been, for Zwingli and Calvin, a *liturgical* preaching service with a pattern for prayer and Scripture, became a *free* preaching service. The sermon was the basic and predominating feature, with lengthy, extemporaneous prayers before and after it. Congregational participation was limited to the singing of metrical psalms in the Reformed church and to German hymns in Lutheran churches. These churches continued to use the prescribed orders for baptism and the Lord's Supper, but the sacraments were rarely celebrated. When these congregations switched from their usual order of prayer, Scripture, prayer, sermon, prayer to a fixed "liturgical" text for the celebration of the sacraments, the very strangeness of the sacramental liturgy tended to reinforce the congregation's impression that the sacraments were something out of the ordinary and foreign to its tradition. When the Lord's Supper was celebrated, it had become an optional appendage to the "regular" Sunday preaching service in the same way as it had been celebrated in the Zwinglian and Free churches.

Why did the Lutherans and the Reformed churches forsake their founders' original intentions and their own heritage and adopt Free Church worship patterns? Many factors are responsible. An overwhelming fear of worship degenerating into a form of "works righteousness" led many Protestants to view worship solely in terms of instruction and moral or spiritual edification of the congregation. The function of the lengthy sermon was to inform the people on matters of correct doctrine and morality. This emphasis on education, on the clear and reasonable word in worship, was compatible with the new Enlightenment stress upon education and verbal communication. The emphasis upon individualism in worship complemented the rise of the capitalist spirit and new democratic, egalitarian ideals.

In other words, that many Protestant liturgical churches in Europe became free worship churches cannot be attributed to the influence of Anabaptists, Puritans, or Independents of the sixteenth century. These groups had mostly migrated to America. In Europe new philosophical and cultural movements were the determining factors.

Rationalism

Discoveries in science and philosophy gave impetus to a movement in thought which characterized the intellectual life of the eighteenth century—the Enlightenment. The Enlightenment attempted to apply the rule of reason to all aspects of life, including religion. (We have already noted some Enlightenment tendencies in the sacramental thought of some of the more radical reformers.) Newton's theories projected a world which operated by law and predictable, understandable patterns. Locke stressed reasonableness as the ultimate test of truth and morality and as the most important aspect of religion. The spread of Rationalism in religion was aided by disgust with the brutalities of the past century of bitter religious wars, dissatisfaction with the narrow and naive biblicism of many Protestants, and resistance to the rigid anti-intellectual reaction of official Roman Catholicism. After all the fighting and bloodshed over religious issues, the rationalists sought a faith which would follow the dictates of moderate, balanced, clear reason rather than "primitive passions."

Rationalism made a great stir in England where Deists sought to reduce religion to a few simple, rational principles free of superstition and narrow-mindedness. Everything that is valuable in Christianity, the Deists argued, is available to us by the use of reason. All that is obscure or beyond proof and reason is mere superstition. Miracles are no real witness to the truth of Christianity and are either superfluous to the faith or are insults to the perfect workmanship and natural order which has been set in place by the Creator.

Inspired by Locke's vision of a harmonious, mechanical, divinely ordered universe, many rationalists looked upon the creation itself as an orderly, verifiable testimony to the validity of faith in God. Joseph Addison (1672-1719) expressed this new natural law theology in a poem which became a popular hymn of the period:

> The spacious firmament on high,
> With all the blue, ethereal sky,
> And spangled heavens, a shining frame,
> Their great Original proclaim:
> Th' unwearied sun, from day to day,
> Does his Creator's power display;
> And publishes to every land
> The work of an almighty hand.
>
> What though, in solemn silence, all
> Move round the dark terrestrial ball?
> What though no real voice nor sound
> Amid their radiant orbs be found?
> In reason's ear they all rejoice,

> And utter forth a glorious voice,
> Forever singing as they shine,
> "The hand that made us is divine."

But in its rather simplistic faith in the sufficiency of "reason's ear," in its deprecation of mystery and feeling in religion, Deism was seen by many as mere, cold-hearted atheism. Deism's popularity was generally limited to England's upper classes and to intellectuals in a few other European countries. In the English colonies of North America, intellectuals like Benjamin Franklin and Thomas Jefferson were among the notable Deists. English Unitarianism, another product of the Enlightenment, swept through English Presbyterian churches during the eighteenth century, calling for new freedom of thought and adherence to reason alone. Unitarianism had a major impact (in a much modified form) upon New England as part of the general rationalizing tendencies of the century.

Among the rationalists the individual conscience, rather than the church's tradition or its corporate experience, was the supreme test of religious truth. Liturgy in general and the sacraments or ordinances in particular were often dismissed by rationalists as anachronistic holdovers from an irrational and superstitious past. The sermon was the only act of worship which was valued by the rationalists, who saw the sermon as a means of inculcating their ideals and of rationally illuminating the enduring truths of reasonable Christianity and universal morality.

Pietism

During the bitter political and theological controversies in Germany, Lutheranism had become solidified into fixed, dogmatic, creedal interpretations of the faith which demanded rigid intellectual conformity. In fighting Lutheran "heresies," "orthodox" Lutherans had emphasized adherence to pure doctrine as the basis for the Christian life rather than the vital relationship between the believer and God which Luther himself had taught. The task of the laity was to understand and to accept these dogmatic statements. Lutheran hymns continued to be sung and appreciated, but the general trend was toward a rather dry Protestant scholasticism.

Pietism broke with these scholastic tendencies, asserted the primacy of emotion in the Christian experience, restored the role of the laity in shaping the church's life, and stressed a strict ascetic attitude toward the world. Pietism was, thus, the antithesis of the rationalism of the age. Pietists like Philipp Jacob Spener (1635-1705) deprecated doctrinal definitions and confessions of faith and exalted personal morality and spirituality. At his home in Frankfort, Pastor Spener gathered a group of like-minded people for Bible reading, prayer, and discussion of Sunday sermons with the aim of deepening the individuals' spiritual lives. His *Pia Desideria* (1675) proposed the formation of small groups, within the larger congregation, which would gather for mutual spiritual edification and encouragement. These *ecclesiola in ecclesia* ("little churches within the church") stressed the ministry of all believers—a Lutheran concept which had been all but forgotten—and the avoidance of doctrinal controversy in favor of an experiential knowledge of religion.

Pietists restored a much-needed dimension to the life of faith. But they also had the effect of placing personal prayer and Bible reading before public worship. Sunday worship tended to be viewed by the Pietists as a kind of psychological experience, a help to the individual believer's religious pilgrimage. Some of Spener's disciples, in spite of his protests, eventually withdrew from church worship and the sacraments altogether.

Pietism also stressed a personal, conscious, experiential conversion experience as the only normal method of entrance into the kingdom of God—a belief which sometimes led them into anti-intellectualism or condemnation of those who failed to duplicate Pietistic conversion patterns. Pietist worship often seemed programmed to produce certain emotional states in the participants.

One of the most notable products of German Pietism was the Moravians, a group of dedicated separatists who became noted for their missionary zeal and their hymnody. An important liturgical contribution of the Moravians was the institution of the "love feast," a joyous meal eaten within the context of corporate worship and stressing Moravian Pietistic ideals of fellowship, warm feeling, and hymn singing.

Methodism and Anglican Evangelicals

The established Church of England, fragmented by the challenges of rationalism, forsaken by the English lower classes, and dissipated by the religious disputes of the preceding century, met the eighteenth century with a spiritual lethargy which was incapable of responding to the needs of the age. In an England on the eve of the industrial revolution, social evils were great: illiteracy, drunkenness, inequalities in the legal system, squalor in the cities, economic victimization.

Early in the century, isolated individuals sought to arouse popular piety. William Law responded to the debilitating influence of Deism with his *Serious Call to a Devout and Holy Life* (1728). By issuing a number of lively and singable hymns between 1690 and 1720, including such favorites as "Joy to the World" and "When I Survey the Wondrous Cross," a Congregationalist, Isaac Watts, challenged Cranmer's notion that no Christian could improve on the Psalms of David. Watts revolutionized English hymnody and assured the centrality of congregational singing in English Free Church worship. Along with individuals like Law and Watts, there were also communal efforts at religious renewal in the form of "religious societies," i.e., small groups of pious Christians who banded together for mutual edification, frequent Communion, study, and social work.

These renewal efforts were mostly sporadic and local in their activity and had little effect. But a great transformation of English religious life was in the making, a mass movement which was finally to affect the religious life of all English people—the Evangelical Revival. The revival began to stir in isolated places throughout England and Scotland in the mid-1700s. But it was only with the emergence of John and Charles Wesley and George Whitefield that the revival took hold.

John and Charles Wesley had both Free Church and Anglican roots. Their grandfathers had been among the ejected Non-Conformist clergy of 1662. But their parents, Samuel Wesley, a country parish pastor, and Susanna Wesley, a remarkably able mother, were devoted Anglicans. First John and then Charles distinguished themselves for scholarship at Oxford. In 1729, Charles Wesley joined a small group of devout Oxford students in founding a club for the purpose of religious reading and frequent Communion. Elder brother John soon became leader of the club. Under John's guidance, the group put into practice William Law's ideals of a consecrated life. They combined social service to local prisoners with High Church Anglicanism. They were also joined by a new student, George Whitefield. Mocking fellow students labeled them "Methodists" because of their advocacy of strict spiritual discipline.

But the club had little influence upon Oxford. Eventually, its members went their separate ways. John Wesley, filled with doubt and turmoil about the insecurity of his own spiritual welfare, sailed with Charles in 1735 to the new colony of Georgia as a missionary to colonists and Indians. The sojourn in Georgia was a disappointment as far as the Wesleys' ministry was concerned. Charles returned home in disgust, and John's punctilious high churchmanship proved unsuited to the needs of the Georgians. In 1738, John returned to England, dismayed by his ineffectiveness.

One of the positive results of the Georgia experience was John Wesley's contact with the Moravians. He was greatly impressed by their deep experiential piety and assurance of their own salvation—an assurance which Wesley himself lacked. But in May of 1738, just a few days after his brother, Charles, had experienced a Moravian-like instantaneous "conversion," John also felt his heart "strangely warmed" while attending a meeting of a religious society on London's Aldersgate Street. John eventually parted with the Moravians because of what he judged to be their exclusivism and subjectivism, but he was forever in their debt for helping to determine a dramatic change in his own life.

John and Charles Wesley now preached a joyful evangelistic message of personal experience of God's love. But when many of their fellow clergy in the established church condemned their "enthusiasm," they were forced to do most of their preaching within the small societies in and around London. George Whitefield even led John into the practice of open-air field preaching to the masses. These open-air sermons, delivered to people who felt excluded from established religion, elicited great response as the Wesleys and Whitefield toured England, bringing their fresh message of God's love to all who would hear.

But the revival might have been simply an occasion for short-lived emotionalism were it not for John's preeminent organizational skills. He formed "societies" as a lay movement within Anglicanism. Cultivated by Wesley's traveling "lay preachers," these societies provided supplementary small group worship experiences, discipline, and settings for "conversions" and social action, all within the context of the established church.

While stressing their new conviction of the necessity for evangelical conversions, the Wesleys also cultivated their love for the *Book of Common Prayer* and the sacraments in the societies. When American Methodists asked him for directives in worship, John Wesley simply made a few minor revisions in the *Book of Common Prayer* and sent it to his "poor sheep in the wilderness," saying he knew of no liturgy "which breathes more of a solid, scriptural, rational Piety." As it turned out, the prayer book seemed ill-suited to American religious needs, and American Methodists mostly ignored it, adopting Free Church worship patterns.

In their stress upon the necessity of frequent Communion, the Wesleys far outdid their contemporaries in the Church of England. As we noted in the last chapter, holy Communion was rarely celebrated in most Anglican parishes. John Wesley himself communed on the average of twice weekly and urged his Methodists to receive the sacrament frequently. The Wesleys shared a generally Calvinist doctrine of the real presence in the sacrament and a high church view of the centrality of both sacraments for the Christian life. Wesleyan eucharistic theology is perhaps best illustrated in Charles Wesley's Communion hymnody *Hymns on the Lord's Supper* (1745), a unique Wesleyan contribution which helped to give Methodist Communions their joyous, evangelistic quality:

> O the depth of love divine,
> Th' unfathomable grace!
> Who shall say how bread and wine
> God into man conveys!
> How the bread his flesh imparts,
> How the wine transmits his blood,
> Fills his faithful people's hearts
> With all the life of God!

John Wesley saw the Lord's Supper as an evangelistic occasion. He had broken with the Moravians, in part, because some of them had asserted that if a person is unsure of one's faith, that person should absent oneself from the sacraments and wait quietly until God renews one's religious hope. Against this "quietist" view, Wesley asserted that Communion is "a justifying as well as a sanctifying ordinance." That is, doubting individuals may be converted to true faith in the very act of participating in the sacrament. "Earnest seekers" were welcome at Wesleyan Communions.

Wesley's dealings with baptism, while consistent with his Anglican heritage, introduced a new element which became a problem for later baptismal practice not only among the heirs of Wesley but also among Protestants in general. True to his Anglican roots, John Wesley believed in the baptismal regeneration of infants. But as a consequence of his own experience, Wesley also affirmed the necessity of later adult evangelical conversion experiences. Wesley appears to have understood later conversion as a kind of renewal, or reawakening, of one's baptism. But he so stressed the importance of adult conversion that later Methodists tended to elevate later conversion at the expense of prior baptism. If baptism needed something more (later evangelical conversion) to complete a person's salvation, how efficacious is baptism? Wesley appeared to hold the two elements together in his own thought, but later Methodists were not as successful. Baptism, particularly infant baptism, was often described by them as a kind of first chapter in God's work with an individual, a first stage which necessitated the completion by the more significant evangelical "conversion." This view had the same effect upon baptismal theology as did the old medieval emphasis upon the necessity of a separate rite of confirmation—it tended to disjoin one element of Christian initiation from another and to suggest that baptism was not the major, effective, sufficient mark of a Christian.

While it was John Wesley's continual desire for his societies to be a force for renewal within the Church of England, as the Methodist societies grew and the number of lay preachers multiplied, pressure arose for authority to administer the sacraments. Wesley resisted this but, in the end, capitulated. The shortage of episcopally ordained men within the movement (particularly in America where Methodism was rapidly growing) and Methodist convictions about the centrality of the Eucharist made his decision almost inevitable. By the time of Wesley's death, Methodism was emerging as a new church even though John and Charles Wesley died as priests in the Church of England.

Wesley, and the general religious revival which he led, gained a number of sympathizers who stayed within the Church of England. These Anglican evangelicals agreed with Wesley's emphases—confident faith, conversion, moral earnestness. Most of these evangelicals tended to be more Calvinist than John Wesley and less inclined to put great emphasis upon sacramental worship, but their movement gave new warmth and liveliness to many Anglican congregations.

Great Awakenings in America

The American counterpart of the eighteenth-century English religious revival was the Great Awakening which began in the 1720s. Coming at a time when conventional patterns of Christian outreach proved unsuited to the particular religious needs of America, and during a period of spreading rationalism, the Awakening emphasized the need for a transforming, regenerative change—a "conversion"—as the normal method of entrance into the church and the faith.

Congregationalist pastor Jonathan Edwards (1703–1758) noted "surprising manifestations of the work of God" among his Massachusetts congregation. George Whitefield swept through the colonies on a series of preaching tours which transformed many communities. When the Methodist movement reached America in the 1760s, it found among the colonists a receptive audience for Wesleyan experiential, evangelical religion. Groups like the Methodists and the Baptists were particularly well suited in polity, doctrine, and temperament to profit from the fervor generated in the Awakening. As the first Awakening ended and the American Revolution began, voluntaristic, evangelical Free churches like the Methodist, Baptist, and Presbyterian were on the eve of what was to be a remarkable century of church growth spurred by continuing "awakenings" and religious revivals. As the nineteenth century began, less than ten percent of the American population were church members. Faced with the challenge of a vast, rapidly growing, unchurched populace, American churches were understandably preoccupied with the winning of converts.

The Second Awakening began in New England as the eighteenth century ended. It spread from there to the Middle Atlantic states, the South, and to frontier states like Kentucky where the most emotional manifestations of the revival were to occur. It was at Cane Ridge, Kentucky, in August of 1801 that one of the most famous frontier camp meetings took place. Here, a crowd estimated at from ten to twenty-five thousand gathered for a week-long revival which was described as "the greatest outpouring of the Spirit since Pentecost." The convenor of the Cane Ridge gathering, a Presbyterian minister named Barton Stone, reported that hundreds of people, upon hearing the gospel, were subject to various kinds of "bodily agitations" which he described as the "jerks," the "dancing exercise," and the "barking exercise." While Stone admitted that "there were many eccentricities, and much fanaticism in this excitement . . . the good effects were seen and acknowledged in every neighborhood." Though some critics charged that "more souls were begot than saved" among the rough frontiersmen who camped at the revival, Cane Ridge was a sign of a revival of revivalism.

In the revivals, preaching and singing were paramount. The message of the evangelist was simple: "Repent and be saved." The goal of the evangelist was limited: conversion of lost souls rather than nurture of the saved. It was worship which focused upon the first steps of faith rather than the long-term sustenance of faith.

A product of the Awakening, Charles Grandison Finney (1792–1875) became known as "the father of modern revivalism." A lawyer by profession, Finney experienced a soul-shaking conversion in 1821 which brought him "a retainer from the Lord Jesus Christ to plead his cause." Refusing formal theological training, Finney immediately began a series of spectacular evangelistic meetings in upstate New York. Advocating certain "new measures," Finney made innovations such as the "anxious bench" to cull from the masses the almost-saved so that they could be better focused upon in prayer and preaching. He encouraged women to testify in public meetings, despite critics who cited Paul (1 Corinthians 14:34) on female silence. He preached in a direct, confrontational, down-to-earth style. Rather than having the people meet at established Sunday worship hours, Finney introduced "protracted meetings" which met for a week or more. Before he entered a town for a revival, he organized his supporters into teams to do advance work, making extensive use of publicity. "A revival is not a miracle," Finney argued against those who charged him with contrived emotional manipulation. ". . . . It is a purely philosophical [i.e., scientific] result of the right use of the constituted means."

The revival represents the greatest single "liturgical" contribution of American Protestantism. It was a creative response to the problem of a vast unchurched populace, a response which was tailored to the needs of a rough, young, and dynamic nation. At its best, it brought the gospel in simple, straightforward terms to those whom established, cautious, conservative churches would probably not have reached. Its songs and hymns were lively, singable, and engaging. For the most part, the black church was born in the age of the revival, where, in the prophetic words of the black preacher and the hope-giving tunes of the spirituals, black people were given hope and determination even in the midst of oppression. Among the white churches, revivalism was a major factor in the great antebellum social reform crusades, social consequences of the passionate, converting vitality of the revival.

One of the most interesting of a number of new Protestant groups which were born in the age of revivals was the Disciples of Christ. In an age of bitter disputes among factions within American Protestantism, the Disciples decided that such divisions are due to "human opinions" which have been added to the simple basic Christian requirements. They resolved to avoid all that the Scriptures avoid. Using this resolve as their guiding principle for reform, they dispensed with creeds, sacraments, and infant baptism. But their biblical emphasis did lead them to recognize the centrality of the Lord's Supper for Christian worship. Disciples therefore recovered weekly celebrations of the Lord's Supper—an anomaly in a time when whatever influence which the Lord's Supper had among most American Free Church Protestants was lessening.

Revivalism was not without its weaknesses, weaknesses which became painfully apparent in American Protestant churches before the end of the nineteenth century. The songs of the revivals, which stressed a simple, direct, heartfelt faith too often led to maudlin, subjective religion. Finney's "new measures," once institutionalized in scores of traveling evangelists and their crusades, became synonymous in the minds of many with religion which is artificially induced, emotionally exploitive, simple-minded, and short-lived. The sermon, ending with a passionate plea to "come to the altar and be saved," was the center of worship, the culmination not only of revivals but of Sunday morning worship also, the supreme goal toward which all other worship acts were merely the "preliminaries." Baptism and the Lord's Supper took a back seat to the supreme "sacrament" of the sermon.

Treatment of the full range of Scripture was woefully inadequate. Prayer became another instrument to achieve the evangelist's objectives. The "pastoral prayer" too often degenerated into a "sermonette with the eyes closed" rather than a pastoral attempt to lead the people to God in prayer. Worship became a means to an end rather than an end in itself. In most Protestant churches, as American preaching went over the same few texts again and again, the transcendent focus of worship was replaced by human-centered worship which resembled a carefully orchestrated preacher-choir performance designed to motivate, titillate, convict, soothe, inspire, or entertain the worshipers rather than to help the worshipers focus upon God.

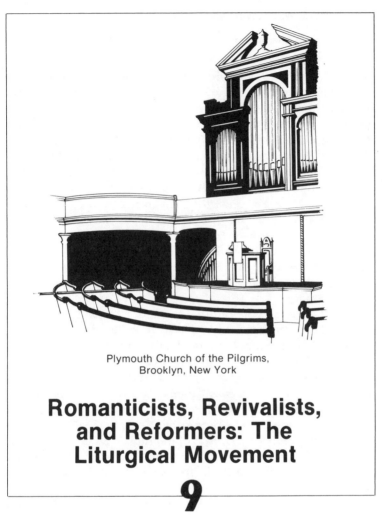

Plymouth Church of the Pilgrims,
Brooklyn, New York

Romanticists, Revivalists, and Reformers: The Liturgical Movement

9

The nineteenth century was an age of revivals. In Europe, the opulent clutter of Victorian architecture gave way to the more severe Gothic Revival. The urbane rationalism of the Enlightenment gave way to extravagant Romanticism. Religious revivals swept across the American frontier fostering the crusading spirit of late nineteenth-century Protestantism. Many of these nineteenth-century revivals became twentieth-century revolutions. In the worship of the Christian church, what began as an effort to revive the old matured into something very new. The Liturgical Movement exemplifies this phenomenon.

The Liturgical Movement Among Roman Catholics

In 1832 a French priest, Prosper Guéranger, along with a handful of ardent priests and laymen, began living the monastic life within the damp ruins of an abandoned priory at Solesmes. It was a peculiarly nineteenth-century act—monks, monasteries, and Gothic ruins stirred the fascination of many Romantics. But Guéranger sought more than escape into the picturesque past. Disgusted by the secularist indifference with which his native France looked upon the demoralized, culturally bound, and sluggish church, Guéranger set out to foster a revitalized Christian institution, centering upon the Mass, which would evangelize a secular society. The historic ability of monasteries to revive civilization attracted Guéranger to primitive monasticism. It seemed to him that the social conditions within which the sixth-century monks lived—social disorder, encroaching barbarism, and a dying culture—were much like the situation in his nineteenth-century France.[1]

To Guéranger, the cardinal sins of the modern age were its "spirit of independence" and "spirit of individuality." The Divine Office had been reduced to a mechanical duty of private clerical devotions. Corporate worship was a minor part of parish life. The spiritual life of the average Roman Catholic in France, and too many other countries, was largely subjective and private in character centering primarily on extraliturgical devotions. Guéranger's monastic community meant to test the principle that liturgy forms individuals into a community. At Solesmes, the Mass was central. The rites and music were perfected so that their beauty would be a public witness to the power of the liturgy and the vitality of the faith.

Solesmes became a center for liturgical research and renewal as the precursor of what became known as the Liturgical Movement. But the work at Solesmes bore the same weaknesses as Guéranger himself. In his reaction against the rationalism and classicism of the eighteenth century, he fell into naive romanticism. He looked upon the Middle Ages as the pinnacle of liturgical

[1] I am indebted to R. W. Franklin, "Guéranger and Pastoral Liturgy: A Nineteenth Century Context," *Worship*, vol. 50, no. 2 (March, 1976), pp. 146-162, for this insight and for background on Guéranger. See also his article "Guéranger: A View on the Centenary of His Death," *Worship*, vol. 49, no. 6 (June-July, 1975), pp. 318-328.

life when the objective power of the liturgy held all in its sway. The Gregorian chant was restored as the best model for liturgical music. Guéranger sought restoration of the "pure Roman rite" and suppression of any local Gallic vestiges in French liturgies. His goal was one of revival rather than renewal or reform. He was only moderately interested in attempts to put the liturgy into the vernacular, believing Latin to be "a veil which protected the mystery of the Mass from the fierce light of every day." He also erroneously believed that the canon was said silently from the beginning. While Guéranger and his cohorts at Solesmes suffered from a lack of critical scholarship and from sentimental "archaeologism," their work led to the great revival of Benedictine liturgical scholarship and opened the door for a serious look at the liturgy as the best witness of the church in the modern world.

Pope Pius X's *Motu proprio* of November 22, 1903, is generally given as marking the date for the birth of the Liturgical Movement. It gave official (if somewhat reserved) sanction to a movement for reform that had begun long before. It spoke of "returning to the fount" of liturgical life and restoring "active participation by the faithful." Specifically, it called for the restoration of the chant as a means of increasing lay participation in the music of worship, more frequent Communion by the faithful within the context of weekly mass, and suggested the need for some future revision of official liturgical books (while warning against rash local liturgical revision).[2]

Dom Lambert Beauduin (1873–1960), a Benedictine monk of Abbey Mont Cesar in Belgium, translated the Roman Missal into the vernacular (for personal reading only) after the papal ban had been lifted in 1897. Retreats for parish choirs were held at Mont Cesar, and semipopular publications for the clergy were printed which stressed the social character of the liturgy as a unifying factor for the church and a means of counteracting the individualism and secularism of the modern world. Dom Beauduin also stressed the teaching function of the liturgy—as primary catechism and a pastoral corrective to the "pious novelties" of much extraliturgical devotion.

The Benedictine Revival spread. In Germany, at the Benedictine Abbey of Maria Laach, Dom Odo Casel's (1886–1948)

[2]Lancelot Sheppard, ed., *The People Worship: A History of the Liturgical Movement* (New York: Hawthorn Books, Inc., 1965), pp. 11, 102-103, 106, 116.

Mysterien theologie ("mystery theology") used Platonic mysticism and Eastern liturgical theology to interpret the sacramental experience to the modern world. Casel claimed that the *mysterium* of Christianity is not the conceptual content of its revelation but, rather, the experience of redemption as we have it made available to us in the liturgical mysteries. As Casel's work spoke to the intellectuals, fellow monk Romano Guardini's *The Spirit of the Liturgy* was a widely circulated interpretation of the liturgy for a popular audience. In 1914, Maria Laach instituted its annual Liturgical Week which trained the laity for liturgical leadership in their local parishes. Also at Maria Laach, Dom Cabrol and Dom Leclercq published a massive encyclopedia on "archaeology and liturgy" which, as a result of better historical work, succeeded in breaking the spell of Romanticism on the Liturgical Movement by shifting the emphasis from medieval to patristic worship standards (The *Apostolic Tradition* of Hippolytus was reconstructed during this period).

In the United States, Benedictines again led the way in the Roman Catholic Liturgical Movement with the founding of the influential magazine *Orate Fratres* in the late twenties (since 1951—*Worship*) at Saint John's Abbey in Collegeville, Minnesota. The first Liturgical Week was held in Chicago in 1940, enabling countless priests and laity to take the fruits of liturgical scholarship to the grass roots. The Liturgical Movement in the United States tended to be more practical and pastoral than intellectual. Here, liturgical revival and the recovery of the ministry of the laity went hand in hand.

Pius XII's *Mediator Dei* (1947), though still cautious, was seen as strong support for the continuing work of the Liturgical Movement. Holy Week services were revised, and the Easter vigil was restored as the central focus of the liturgical year. Experiments in the vernacular for occasional services were authorized. Some requirements for preparatory fasting for the Eucharist were lifted, and the celebration of major rites at evening hours was authorized in an attempt to meet the needs of modern working people.

The first order of business at Vatican II was reform of the liturgy, and it became clear that the reform would be sweeping and even somewhat radical. But the Roman church had not come to this stage overnight—Vatican II was the culmination of renewal which had been initiated long before.

The Liturgical Movement Among Protestants

For Protestants, the Liturgical Movement frequently meant the recovery of the liturgical norms of the Reformation, the discovery that Protestant forebears were not as "protestant" as was once assumed. Luther and Calvin's eucharistic emphasis was brought to light by Protestant liturgical studies, and the Reformation—sidetracked by pietism, subjectivism, rationalism, and revivalism—continued its work of liturgical reform.

Lutherans renewed their interest in Luther's liturgical thought as a counterforce to the impact of later German Pietism. The Bach Chorale was reclaimed as a distinctive Protestant contribution to liturgical music. In this century Rudolf Otto, philosopher and mystic, wrote *The Idea of the Holy* which, despite its subjectivistic approach, was to prove helpful in translating worship theology to a contemporary church which hungered for a respite from the dull didacticism of Protestant worship. Friedrich Heiler's "High Church Lutheranism" of the 1920s fostered a new ecumenical spirit among Lutherans. The Liturgical Institute, founded at Valparaiso University in 1949, fostered liturgical renewal in Lutheran churches throughout the United States.

Among the Reformed (Calvinist) churches, a new interest in Calvin's liturgical thought surfaced in the mid-1800s. As with the Lutherans, many Reformed pastors were surprised at the liturgical views of their forebear, Calvin. Scholars in the Church of Scotland, like D. H. Hislop, D. M. Baillie, and W. D. Maxwell, sparked an interest in richer, more formal, more traditional (in the true Calvinist sense) worship as a way of reviving the somewhat dry, verbose, didactic worship in which many Reformed churches languished.

Unlike the usual pattern for liturgical renewal in other bodies, some of the earliest ferment in Reformed worship came, not from Europe, but from the United States. Charles W. Baird's *Eutaxia* (1855) hit like a bombshell among American Calvinists. Baird brought to light the long suppressed liturgies of Calvin, Knox, and other Reformed leaders. In the 1840s and 1850s, the Mercersburg Movement blossomed at the German Reformed Seminary in Pennsylvania under the scholarly leadership of J. W. Nevin (1803-1886) and Philip Schaff (1819-1893). Nevin's *The Mystical Presence* set forth a Reformed eucharistic theology. He was a strong opponent of Charles G. Finney's "new measures" which

Nevin accused of transforming American Protestant worship into blatant emotional manipulation in its attempt to use worship to motivate participants to "make a decision for Christ." Schaff, a distinguished church historian, charged that American evangelicalism's exclusivistic focus on sin neglected the proper focus of worship—namely, the grace of God. Nevin felt that praise and adoration, central acts of historic Christian worship, had become submerged in pulpit-pounding rhetoric and trivial moralizing. While the Mercersburg Movement was tinged with the same romanticism and antiquarianism that colored the Liturgical Movement elsewhere during this period, its seeds were to bear fruit in the next century's reforms. Henry Van Dyke led a revision of the liturgy in the Presbyterian Church (U.S.A.) in 1931, which showed a recovery of Calvin's legacy as well as debts to Anglican and Lutheran works.

While European Reformed churches were slower in liturgical renewal, the Protestant monks of Taizé in France became a fascinating example of Protestant worship which was heavily influenced by Roman Catholic liturgical trends. The Swiss Reformed biblical scholar, Oscar Cullmann, investigated the biblical basis of sacramental theology and gave Protestants a new appreciation for the centrality of liturgy to the composition and message of the Bible. Too many Protestants had forgotten that the Bible was a worship text itself! Cullmann's studies were part of a general reawakening of the old Protestant interest in the Bible as guide and source for liturgical renewal.[3]

Anglicanism showed the heaviest involvement in the Liturgical Movement. A revival of "high church" sentiments accompanied the loss of fire among Anglican evangelicals, a reaction against the austerity of Calvinism, plainness of Puritanism, and the rise of Romanticism. What might be lumped together as the Tractarian-Oxford-Anglo-Catholic-Ritualist movement swept through Anglicanism in the late 1800s. Edward Pusey (1800–1882) sought to reunite the English and Roman churches by stressing Anglicanism's Roman roots in worship and theology. Pusey's friend, John Henry Newman (1801–1890), eventually became a Roman Catholic and a cardinal. John Keble (1792–1866) stressed Anglo-Catholicism as an antidote to the frightening

[3] Oscar Cullmann, *Early Christian Worship,* trans. A. Stewart Todd and James B. Torrance (London: SCM Press Ltd., 1953).

declension of denominations in Britain. Keble left a legacy of hymns and poems for the liturgical year. Edward Irving (1792–1834) left the Scottish Presbyterians and founded the "Holy Catholic Apostolic Church" in 1832 which combined ritualism; bits of Greek, Anglican, and Roman liturgies; millenarianism; and apocalypticism in a strange brew of nineteenth-century religious infatuations. In music, Edward Caswell (1814–1878) and John Mason Neale (1818–1866) diligently recovered Greek and Latin hymns and urged their use in English liturgy.

In architecture, Augustus Pugin (1812–1852) led the Gothic Revival, seeing the Gothic style as the golden age of church architecture. The table, brought out to the people by the reformers, was restored to its medieval position against the apsidal wall. The choir was elevated on a stagelike setting between the people and the table. The table eventually became an impressive, remote sideboard, cluttered with crosses, flowers, and candles. Rood screens, processional crosses, and public reservation of the sacrament were other ritualistic additions to Anglican worship during this period, along with eucharistic vestments, mitres, copes, tippets, and stoles. The once austere Cranmerian Anglican houses of worship were transformed into dark neo-Gothic interiors accented with new paraments which borrowed Baroque Roman liturgical color schemes. As in many other manifestations of the Liturgical Movement, the Anglican liturgical revival was not without its romanticism, antiquarianism, clericalism, and aestheticism.

"Evangelicals" within the Anglican communion fought the "Ritualists" over these Gothic revivals, with excesses on both sides of the argument. The movement did break the rigid uniformity that had characterized Anglican worship in the eighteenth and early nineteenth centuries and opened up Anglicanism to a more comprehensive use of its liturgical past. The movement made the church appealing in a new way to those who were repelled by the arid, intellectualized, and stiflingly formalized use of the *Book of Common Prayer* into which Anglicanism had withdrawn following its struggle with dissenting factions. A score of prominent Anglican liturgiologists had their roots in this period—Brightman, Frere, Srawley, and Dix, to mention a few. The round of prayer book revisions in the 1920s in England, Scotland, Canada, South Africa, and the United States was the fruit of the movement in Anglicanism. Throughout this period and its prayer book revisions, the rites themselves were changed less than the ceremonial, liturgical piety, and theology which surrounded the rites.

Among Free Church-oriented Protestants in America, the early nineteenth-century revivals had become institutionalized as the pattern for Sunday worship. Influenced by the phenomenal growth of the more radically Protestant groups (i.e., Southern Baptists), and nurtured in an environment which always bore a deep suspicion of Old World "ritualism" and "formalism" as opposed to emotional "spontaneity" and "freedom" in worship, many Free Church American Protestants saw the Liturgical Movement, as it began to infiltrate their churches in the twentieth century, not as a revival but, rather, as a decline and a denial of a once vibrant evangelical fervor.

Ironically, both the Liturgical Movement and American revivalism stressed recovery of emotion even though the two movements were at odds as to how to revive emotion in worship and what the focus and content of the emotion were. American Free Church Protestantism had lost the Eucharist as a focal point for corporate life. Indeed, in the voluntaristic, congregationalist, democratic American environment, corporate worship was often sacrificed to aggressive individualism in American religious life as had been the case in American business life. In claiming to be not of the world, American evangelicalism with its pragmatic, utilitarian, businesslike crusades and Madison Avenue-like revivals had begun to look very much like the surrounding culture.

Baptism, like the Eucharist, was emptied of much of its sacramental meaning for those whose forebears had regarded baptism as a sacrament. American Protestants had waged heated battles over baptism in the nineteenth century and now sought unity, often by assuring themselves that theological niceties surrounding baptism and the Lord's Supper were of little consequence anyway. Among most Methodists and Presbyterians, Zwinglian views had replaced their historic positions on the sacraments. Baptism was overshadowed by later or prior evangelical conversion experiences. Revivalism elevated one's personal religious experience over corporate acts of worship or sacramental means of grace. The Word—read, preached, taught, personally experienced, and personally affirmed—was more important to most American Protestants than the sacraments and other corporate worship activities. Reinhold Niebuhr noted that American Methodism ". . . has no theology, only dissipated evangelical fervor" and that, as a whole, American Protestantism's

> protest against the various forms and disciplines [of worship] led to their destruction. It may be possible to have a brief period of religious spontaneity in which the absence of such disciplines does not matter. The evangelism of the American frontier may have been such a period. But this spontaneity does not last forever. When it is gone a church without adequate conduits of traditional liturgy and theological learning and tradition is without the waters of life.[4]

Increasing numbers of American Protestants in the Free Church tradition were becoming dissatisfied with their worship patterns as the twentieth century began. In the 1920s, as the "liturgical churches" became more involved in the Liturgical Movement, many main-line Protestant denominations saw efforts among some of their constituents to "enrich" worship. Methodist Bishop Wilbur P. Thirkield, writing in a 1932 issue of the Federal Council of Churches *Bulletin,* claimed the issue was not a question of more ritual but

> rather the securing of a sense of the presence of God in the service of the sanctuary. The lack of a spirit of orderly and devout conduct of the service and reverence in worship is a weakness in great numbers of our churches. Men crave to hear the note of eternity in the sanctuary.[5]

Too often, Protestant worship reformers confounded the psychological with the theological, exchanging the old emotional manipulation of the pulpit-pounding revival with new manipulation by use of candles, crosses, and paraments. George Walter Fiske, in urging his fellow Protestants to break with the "Puritan tradition," wrote in 1931:

> More beautiful churches, more worshipful music, more use of suggestive symbolism, the adoption of the chancel with its real aids to worship, the pageantry of the processional with the dignity of vestments, all furnish a vastly more . . . psychological appeal to . . . the whole personality, instead of to intellect and conscience only.[6]

[4] Reinhold Niebuhr, *Essays in Applied Christianity,* ed. D. B. Robertson (New York: Meridian Books, imprint of The World Publishing Company, 1959), p. 62.
[5] Quoted in Massey Hamilton Shepherd, Jr., ed., *The Liturgical Renewal of the Church* (New York: Oxford University Press, 1960), p. 58.
[6] George Walter Fiske, *The Recovery of Worship* (New York: Macmillan, Inc., 1931), p. 233.

Undoubtedly, the quest to "enrich worship" was related to the growing economic power and rising educational and cultural level of American society in this century.

Sometimes worship reform was pushed by proponents of liberal theology who sought to break out of the old worship patterns in order to find a more suitable liturgical expression for their beliefs. Social gospel worship aids like Rauschenbusch's *Prayers of the Social Awakening* (1910) and Washington Gladden's and Frank Mason North's hymns influenced Protestants, particularly the Methodists, and helped to turn Protestant worship away from its subjectivistic individualism to a more corporate, worldly action. The weakness in the liberal approach to worship was that it tended to reduce worship to a means of rallying Christians to social action. It continued the former revivalistic view of worship as a means of motivating people to do something, a means of doing something to or for people rather than an activity directed toward God. In this vein, the Federal Council of Churches instituted a new season for the church year, "Kingdomtide," in which social gospel themes of kingdom building and service to humanity would be lifted up in worship. The new season took hold only among the Methodists.

There were more specific manifestations of the Liturgical Movement's influence among American Protestants. The "Open" or "divided chancel" (in protest against the pulpit-centered arrangement) with its accompanying chancel rail and altar with a reredos or dossal curtain was introduced as the architectural focus of attention. Vestments were worn first by the choir and then by the clergy. Methodist and Congregationalist clergy, claiming their Anglican heritage, donned cassock, surplice, and plain stoles keyed to the colors of the liturgical year. The cross, once considered a popish anathema in many Protestant circles, was introduced in neo-Gothic fashion atop the newly installed altars along with a host of new symbols to "enrich" the "sanctuary." The Hymn Society of America, founded in 1922, and the School of Sacred Music at Union, founded in 1928, helped train Protestant music leaders who labored to introduce traditional and new hymns which stressed the adoration and majesty of God in corporate worship over the old subjectivism of the popular revival and gospel songs. The seasons of the church year were recovered along with lectionary Bible readings (which fit nicely into the widely influential biblical theology movement of this period) as two means of introducing a wider variety of worship and preaching themes. New Protestant service books were published, offering rich worship resources and full orders of worship. Finally, liturgical revival went hand in hand with the growing spirit of ecumenism. Many Protestants discovered that liturgy often united separated Christian groups where discussions on doctrine and polity had failed.

Not all Protestants welcomed this new liturgical interest, suspecting a forsaking of evangelical fervor and a backsliding into "popish traditions." Modern Pentecostalism, with its emphasis on the descent of the Spirit and "unknown tongues," was, in part, a rebellion against "lifeless forms" in Protestant worship. Neo-orthodoxy, the dominant theology of post-World War II main-line Protestantism, centered itself around "The Word" of preaching as the primary focus of divine-human encounter. Existentialism, and its attendant theological formulations in the theologies of men like Paul Tillich and Rudolf Bultmann, manifested subjectivistic, individualistic tendencies which militated against renewal of corporate worship or sacramental emphasis. "Christ meets us in the word of preaching and nowhere else," Bultmann flatly declared.

Protestants had not yet developed, as the Roman Catholics had, sufficient theological basis for their liturgical reforms. Too many innovations were superficial, borrowed adornments without any doctrinal or historical grounding. Protestants had allowed others to do their "homework" for them. Too often, Protestants had haphazardly borrowed aesthetic enrichments from other traditions without coming to terms with their own distinct witness in worship, to the end result that for the average Protestant, worship remained an adjunct activity of the Christian life. Baptism and the Lord's Supper were mere symbols of prior individualistic religious experience—water and wine and bread were still subservient to the Word. And yet—a revival had begun.

Innovation, Creation, Consensus: Present and Future

10

Godfrey Diekmann, editor of *Worship,* recalls that, during Vatican II, as liturgical reforms were being debated late one evening, one of the East German bishops reminded the Council of something we Christians at times forget—the importance of corporate worship for the church.

The bishop noted that the Communists have their own highly developed pseudoliturgies which glorify the state and its power, acts of state worship which seek to outshout Christian liturgy. In his country, the government had abolished all church societies and Christian educational gatherings. The only thing the Catholics had left was Sunday Mass. The bishop then begged the Council to be as radical as it could in its revision of the church's rites, especially the Sunday Eucharist, so that the Mass could again become an experience of common identity, shared faith, and Christian hope for his people. After the bishop's pleas, the worship reforms of the Council were rapid and far-reaching. Vatican II signaled the maturing of the Liturgical Movement into a new, worldwide, ecumenical effort to recover the corporate character of the community at worship.

Wherever Christians gather this Sunday, in whatever circumstances they find themselves, there is a growing appreciation for the centrality of congregational worship, a growing awareness that if our faith is not proclaimed and enacted in Sunday worship, if we do not receive our identity and mandate in this time of praise and thanksgiving, it is unlikely that we will receive these gifts elsewhere.

Emerging Ecumenical Consensus

One of the sad facts of church history is our tendency to express, even to accentuate, the painful divisions in the Body of Christ through our worship. While the bitterness of our past arguments over baptism, the Lord's Supper, ordination, and prayer show how significant these activities are for us, their significance has often been perverted to serve as an occasion for separation rather than unity. But developments in recent years have changed this situation as far as the church's worship is concerned.

Study of the history of the liturgy has been a major contributor to the emerging ecumenical consensus on worship. Old arguments, when placed in context, have been put aside in favor of more fruitful dialogue. In returning to our heritage in worship, we have been continually impressed by our commonality rather than our differences. In stripping away accumulated liturgical bric-a-brac, we now see more clearly the most basic, shared elements of Christian worship. As a result, churches which have been unable to achieve doctrinal or political unity now find that they are able to join hands over the word, water, and wine and bread.

In chapter 9 we noted how, as the Liturgical Movement matured, a number of factors contributed to the growing consensus on worship. The renewed interest in biblical studies helped to move us back to our common book. While the Bible cannot be used as a simple guidebook of liturgical directives (as we learned in the Reformation), it is the final measure of our faithfulness and helps to remind us of the variety, richness, simplicity, and communal nature of Christian worship from its beginning.

The rediscovery of patristic worship material from the first centuries of the church has had an immense influence upon worship reform. In chapter 3, when the *Apostolic Tradition* was discussed, we noted Hippolytus's influence upon all liturgical revisions since the 1930s. The simplicity, conciseness, and clearly discernible patterns of patristic worship were most appealing when these early practices were compared with some of our later and more disordered rites. We learned again that Christian worship is not so much a set of words and fixed written texts but, rather, a pattern of basic actions which allow for possible variations in the words. We received a more objective, balanced view of Reformation and Counter-Reformation developments by moving past these arguments to a period before these divisive and unproductive arguments began. Hippolytus brought us back to our roots, to a time when the Eucharist was the central, constitutive, crucial activity of every Sunday and when baptism was a radical, transforming process of conversion into a radically changed community of faith.

In studying the history of the Reformation, we Protestants rediscovered our own worship roots and, in the process, found that some of our forebears had worship ideas which were counter to our present practices. The eucharistic and baptismal theology of Calvin and Luther found our current views of the sacraments wanting. Increased contacts through ecumenical conversations led to increased borrowing from one another's traditions for a mutual enriching of one another's worship life.

Cultural changes, the unintelligibility of archaic liturgical language, new versions of the Bible, different views of the church and its mission, and the growing voice of the ethnic churches all contributed to growing pressure to change our worship in the sixties and seventies. New liturgies were written. Local congregations experimented with dialogue sermons, multimedia worship, liturgical dance, folk music, increased congregational participation, drama, and a wide variety of other experiences that would have been deemed inappropriate for Christian worship only a decade before. Part of the purpose of this book has been to suggest that many of these changes have come about, not simply from boredom with the old and infatuation with the new, but because of a new awareness of the history of our worship. Historical study of the liturgy enables us to criticize intelligently the old and the new, to distinguish between what is essential and what is merely peripheral or what is inconsistent and even unfaithful. In this period of liturgical experimentation, historical study helps us judge between responsible innovation and mere gimmickry. We are motivated, in both our study and our experimentation, by a desire to return to the sources, to recover the vitality and richness which many of us lost in our worship life over the years, and to allow our past to inspire us to sing again "a new song unto the Lord" in our own time and place.

James White has noted that some of the most radical changes have occurred in Communions which were once considered to be the most liturgically conservative—Roman Catholics, Lutherans, Episcopalians. Perhaps this is because they have the security of a solid historical background. Too many Protestants are not quite sure where "home" is; so they are reluctant to stray far in their experiments. The Roman Catholic, on the other hand, has the security of knowing that, no matter how far the congregation ranges in its worship, there is always the solid security of "home." Sometimes historical knowledge gives us the confidence to be more innovative.

But whatever our individual Communion, whatever the current state of reform within our own tradition, there is an emerging ecumenical consensus about Christian worship—where we have been and where we ought to be headed—which is destined to influence the worship life of every Christian church. Let us close with a very brief summary of the major aspects of that consensus.

Christian Initiation

The old practice of infant baptism assumed that secular society was a prop for the church. Today there is broad agreement that if the church was ever justified in assuming that birth into society in general was also birth into the Christian community, it can no longer do so. In the new baptismal rites, particularly those of Lutherans, United Methodists, Roman Catholics, and Episcopalians, there is a new seriousness about baptism as a radical, life-changing, revolutionary experience of conversion into the faith and initiation into the household of God.

In recent ecumenical discussions of baptism, there has been broad agreement on the necessary preconditions for a full, normative baptism.

1. *Water.* We have seen, in the history of Christian initiation, a reduction in the amount of water used in the rite. We thereby cut ourselves off from the full range of rich biblical imagery related to the waters of baptism. New baptismal rites stress the abundant use of water. Water should be seen, heard, and experienced in order to open up the rich baptismal symbolism. Among Protestants, this means a new appreciation for the power of the visible, concrete, tangible symbols of our faith, an appreciation which our Enlightenment rationality and fixation with the Word has long obscured.

2. *A responding person.* Baptism signifies to all not only that the initiate has been adopted, initiated, and accepted into the household of faith but also that the initiate has accepted and responded to that adoption. The new baptismal rites use pre- and post-baptismal instruction and responsive creeds during baptism to underscore the initiate's response. There is a new seriousness that baptism should be a truly converting and nurturing activity. Christian initiation is defined more as a lifelong process of conversion and growth than as a once-and-for-all rite. While churches which have previously baptized infants will probably continue to do so, there is emerging agreement among liturgical scholars that an adult initiate is the norm for baptism. The norm for the new rites is adult initiation, with suggested variations in the rites for the baptism of children and infants of Christian parents. In churches where infants of Christian parents are baptized, special care needs to be taken to insure that full response into the faith is nurtured within the baptized child. At whatever age a person is baptized, there is a growing awareness that baptism is the beginning rather than the end of the Christian pilgrimage. While the old rite of "confirmation" is somewhat deemphasized (because it tends to fragment Christian initiation and detract from the efficacy of baptism), most of the new baptismal rites make provision for periodic baptismal festivals within the life of the church when members of the congregation are given the opportunity to renew their baptismal vows and to continue to

grow in their awareness of what it means to be claimed by God and God's church in baptism. The old rite of confirmation can best be interpreted as one of these later opportunities for baptismal renewal. The basic question for all of us, in regard to baptism, is not so much, "How old should someone be before he or she is baptized?" Rather, the basic issue is, "What kind of church do we want and what is the best way to form that church by our initiation into the church?"

3. Above all, a full, normative baptism requires that baptism be done *within the context of the believing, witnessing community*. It is the church which bears Christ's command to go into all the world, baptizing and teaching. Past arguments over the proper age of baptism or the requisite beliefs or life-style required for baptism have obscured the fact that our primary concern in baptism should be upon the church and God working through the church rather than upon the recipient of baptism. The main burden of faith and action is upon the baptizers. It is the church which bears the responsibility of making disciples. The new rites strongly discourage baptisms without the presence of the full, worshiping congregation. The rites provide many opportunities for congregational participation (congregational sponsors of baptismal candidates, lay instruction of candidates, congregational responses and prayers during the service). The congregation's presence reminds us that the Christian faith is a family affair—not an isolated, individualized experience. We are encouraged to celebrate baptism within the context of the Lord's Supper so that baptism will be more clearly seen as entrance into the family's fellowship as we move from font to table. If baptism is the beginning of a lifelong process of conversion and nurture, then the church, at any baptism, assumes lifelong responsibility for the conversion and nurture of the person being baptized. The presence and participation of the church in the rite of baptism is also a reminder to the baptizand that the Christian faith involves initiation into a family with all the rights and responsibilities of family life. Baptism is a yoking of oneself to a specific gathering of the Body of Christ, not an abstracted, free-floating initiation into religion in general or an occasion for mere self-affirmation.

The Service of the Word

The Divine Office—the noneucharistic service of prayer,

Scripture, and preaching—followed a circuitous route during the Reformation and emerged as the most popular and most frequently celebrated Sunday service within Protestantism. It has, from its beginning, been heavy on words and light on actions and genuine congregational participation. It offers the advantage of covering a wide range of biblical material with directness and simplicity. It has been widely used, especially in Protestantism, as a time for congregational instruction, nurture, and motivation. It is here that the Service of the Word, "Eleven O'Clock Worship Hour," or whatever a church calls it, has been most abused. While edification and instruction always occur when the Christian community gathers for worship, the primary purpose of our worship is always praise and prayer which are directed to God, not edification and instruction directed to the community. In our Protestant, Sunday morning "preaching service," there is a great need to examine the focus, purpose, and direction of our worship. Whenever that service is *used* to motivate the congregation to respond to the denomination's latest program, or the pastor's own crusade, or social action, or personal commitment—or to educate, titillate, soothe, excite, coerce—or any other often worthwhile purpose, then it is safe to say that the worship of God has been perverted into a means of achieving our own human purposes rather than an occasion to respond to God's purposes. This is less than full Christian worship.

In looking at the history of the Divine Office, or Service of the Word, and in evaluating the state of this service in our churches today, there is broad agreement that a number of inadequacies need to be corrected.

1. The Service of the Word, or any other Sunday morning gathering of the church for worship, is not primarily an occasion for private worship. This is a public, corporate occasion. The service should draw us more fully into the Body of Christ rather than provide occasion for us to withdraw more deeply into ourselves. Corporate singing, corporate prayer, and corporate actions are the way to achieve truly corporate worship.

2. A related concern is the woeful lack of lay involvement and leadership in most of our worship. Oftentimes Free Church Protestants, who speak the most about the "priesthood of all believers," are the most guilty of promoting clergy-dominated worship in which the minister does all the preaching, praying,

speaking, acting, and leading, and the people do all the passive sitting and listening. We can do more on Sunday morning to lift up the ministry of *all* Christians in our worship, not just the ministry of the ordained Christians.

3. All too many of our Sunday services are poorly structured without any understandable connection between the various acts of worship. There is no "flow" or logical movement in the service. An insufficient amount of Scripture is read. The sermon has little relation to the service as a whole, the seasons of the church year, or even the Scripture lessons. Prayers are poorly constructed and weak on solid content. The Psalter is haphazardly used and indifferently read. Hymns, choir, and organ music appear to have no relation to the themes, events, or content of the rest of the service. And, to return to an earlier concern, there is insufficient opportunity for congregational response within the service.

4. Finally, the most basic problem with the Service of the Word is that many of us are attempting to make this service do a task which it was never intended to do. We have tried to make it the basic, full, normal Sunday service for Christians. We have tried to elevate the sermon to the level of a supreme sacrament which must bear the total burden of the congregation's judgment, grace, healing, nourishment, response, and edification upon its shoulders. But if our survey of Christian Sunday worship over the centuries has convinced us of anything, it has shown us that the basic, full, normal Sunday service for Christians, in "all times and places," has been the full service of Word *and* Table. When we do not move from the Service of the Word to the Service of the Table, we are cheating ourselves of the full range of Christian experience. We are going through the historic acts of preparation for the experience of table fellowship without actually experiencing it. This often gives our Sunday worship a truncated quality. Congregational responsiveness continues to be a problem among those of us for whom the full service of Word and Table is only rarely celebrated because congregational movement to the Lord's Table is *the* primary, biblical, historical response to the read, prayed, and preached Word.

For most of us Free Church Protestants, this means that our primary, biblical, historical agenda for worship renewal is the recovery of the centrality and the frequent celebration of the Lord's Supper in our churches.

The Service of the Table

In recent thought on the history, theology, and practice of the Lord's Supper, or the Eucharist, four central themes have emerged which have received amazingly broad agreement among both Protestant and Roman Catholic scholars.

1. As stated above, a full service of Word *and* Table is the normal Sunday morning activity for Christians. The recovery of the Lord's Supper as a frequently celebrated Sunday event is imperative.

2. In our celebrations of the Lord's Supper, our prayers, hymns, and actions should focus upon the entire saving work of Christ—his birth, healing, passion, teaching, death, resurrection, ascension, and present reign—not simply upon the somber meal in the upper room. The Lord's Supper is not some doleful memorial for a lost hero. It is a joyous victory celebration for a resurrected and reigning Lord. Sunday is the day of resurrection. The new prayers recover this joyful, celebrative quality and treat a variety of Christological themes, unlike many of our Reformation prayers which refer only to Jesus' words and actions in the upper room.

3. The Lord's Supper is the communal, corporate act of the church *par excellence.* The joy of communal fellowship with Christ and with the members of the Body of Christ is its goal more than individualistic, self-centered, heavily penitential introspection. Sunday is the day for Communion and community rather than a day for one's private meetings with God.

4. As the central symbolism of water is being recovered in our renewal of baptism, so the central symbolism of a meal is being recovered in our renewal of the Lord's Supper. Real leavened bread and real wine should be offered, blessed, and given in sufficient quantities so as to lift up the full, rich, and wide-ranging symbolism of a common meal where the host is Christ himself. Many congregations are recovering the joy and the vivid symbolism of using a common cup and a common loaf of home-baked bread. We Protestants are learning again to trust the old, biblical symbols rather than rely exclusively upon words. We are learning again that the Lord's Supper is something which is done—tasted, touched, smelled, and acted—rather than something which is only spoken and heard.

In the final analysis, the current worship reform movement is not so much concerned with the reform of the liturgy as with the renewal of the church. It arises from a conviction that worship is central to the life and mission of the church.

So the question is not: Which age or rite of baptism is best? The question is: How do we best make Christians? The question is not: Which method of preaching is most enticing to modern listeners? The question is: In this time and place, how is the story best told and the word best proclaimed? The question is not: How often do we celebrate the Lord's Supper, or what text is best for the Eucharist? The question is: How do we nourish Christians?

We ask the questions in confidence that, when asked with boldness and faithfulness, God will give us the answers. So may our prayer and praise, in our time and place, join with all the saints who, at all times and places, have reached out to God in worship, only to find God was, at all times and places, reaching out to them.

Index

Agape, 23-24
Anabaptists, 71f., 87, 93
Anamnesis (Remembrance), 37f., 47
Apostles' Creed, 32, 59, 65
Apostolic Tradition. See Hippolytus
Architecture, 40f., 111, 114

Baptism, 25ff., 34, 39, 44f., 70, 71, 83, 92, 112, 121f.
  infant, 26f., 33, 45, 58f., 67, 71, 78, 100
Baptists, 86f.
Beauduin, Dom Lambert, 107
Berekah, 36

Black church worship, 103
Book of Common Prayer, 77ff., 99
Bucer, Martin, 70

Calvin, John, 67, 69f., 73f., 76, 92, 109
Chaburah, 18-19
Christian initiation. *See* Baptism
Christological controversies (4th century), 43f.
Clergy, 34, 42
Confirmation, 32, 44f., 59f., 67, 83
Constantine, 39f., 45
Cranmer, Thomas, 76ff., 97

127